FLOWERS AND GARDENS

A Manual for Beginners

Flowers and Gardens

Floriculture is cultivation of flowers and becoming and value added farm income to the farmers. Flowers are being considered for the peace, harmony and respect. Now a days, it has taken a shape of industry. Moreover, the Indian especially housewives and senior citizens grow flowers or flowering plants in pots or in the open yards. The cultivation of cut flowers and potted plants is widely spread throughout the world. The consumption of flowers has increased with the increase in standard of livings.

The book"Flowers and Gardens" gives a detail account on the cultivation of various types of flowers, their maintenance and protection from insect pests and diseases.

This book is very useful for the beginners who are interested in potted flowers and gardening, if commercially grows, the book is quite helpful to the growers.

FLOWERS AND GARDENS

A Manual for Beginners

R. TEMPLE-WRIGHT

BIOTECH
2023
Biotech Books

ISBN 81-7622-099-X

Published by : **BIOTECH BOOKS**
4762-63/23, Ansari Road, Darya Ganj,
New Delhi - 110002
Phones : 011 4300 3222
Email : biotechbooks@yahoo.co.in

PRINTED IN INDIA

PREFACE

In preparing this edition for the press, I wish to thank those whose enthusiastic reception of preceding editions has led to the speedy necessity for a fourth.

Even in its present form which has grown considerably since the first edition - it does not presume to be more than a manual for beginners, but the importance of a *good beginning* lies in the fact of its being the best assurance of a successful ending, so once again I have great pleasure in encouraging everyone to *begin* to garden. After that, industry, taste and imagination will open to you the gates of an earthly paradise.

R. Temple-Wright

The Dial of Flowers

'Twas a lovely thought to mark the hours,
   As they floated in light away,
By the opening and the folding flowers,
   That laugh to the summer's day.

Thus had each moment its own rich hue,
   And its graceful cup and bell,
In whose coloured vase might sleep the dew,
   Like a pearl in an ocean shell.

To such sweet signs might the time have flowed
   In a golden current on,
Ere from the garden, man's first abode,
   The glorious guests were gone.

So might the days have been brightly told –
   Those days of song and dreams –
When shepherds gathered their flocks of old
   By the blue Arcadian streams.

So, in those isles of delight, that rest
   Far off in a breezeless main,
Which many a bark with a weary guest
   Has sought, but still in vain.

Yet is not life, in its real flight,
   Marked thus - even thus - on earth,
By the closing of one hope's delight
   And another's gentle birth?

Oh! let us live so that, flower by flower,
   Shutting in turn, may leave
A lingerer still for the sunset hour
   A charm for the shaded eve.

Hemans.

FLOWERS AND GARDENS

Pleasures of Gardening

"Gardening has been the inclination of kings, the choice of philosophers, the common favourite of public and private men; a pleasure of the greatest, and the care of the meanest; and indeed, an employment and a possession for which no man too high or too low." – *Sir William Temple*

A little talk about Gardening

If you were to receive a letter, the envelope of which was dirty, torn and disreputable, would you not feel disgusted. And would your disgust disappear entirely if, inside that dirty envelope, you found a letter written on dainty, scented paper?

At least, you could not get over the incongruity between the covering an its contents. In the same way, only to a much greater degree, does one feel the difference of attention bestowed on the outside and on the inside of many of the bungalows in which we live in India. Then let us try to make the exterior of our houses a little more in keeping with the interior, let the beauty of the garden harmonise with the dainty taste of the drawing-room.

The general excuse all over India is –

"Oh! but we may be here such a short time, so what is the use of bothering?" Yes, we are all moved about more or less, but, if one Virgil's principle - "Sow you, not for yourselves"- each of us improved the look of the ground outside our doors, and did even a little gardening, we should leave behind for our successors in one station only what they would have got ready for us in the other to which we are transferred, so, you see, we should give no more than we mean to take! Well, now that we are agreed, the outside of our dwellings shall not illustrate the well-known lines –

"I passed by his garden and saw the wild brier.

The thorns and the thistless grow broader and higher."

let us set to work and make a beginning. Decide how much of your ground you can afford to cultivate as a flower garden, then enclose this with a hedge which will be ornamental as well as useful. See *Camphire, Dodonea* and *Inga dulcis,* all extremely nice for the purpose. You will find the love of gardening grow upon you, and you will by-and-bye want to enlarge your boundary, so it will be best, at the very first, to leave a margin of ground for this after enlargement. Mark your line of hedge and set about it in the hot weather, and at the same time mark where your lawn, shrubbery, rosary, &c., are to be, and clear these places as recommended under those heads.

Laying out the Ground

We must do this in the *quickest,* the least expensive and the simplest way.

Let us see whether there is any ground to make a garden and then let us "clean up" round the house *first.* One or two coolies must be got to clear away every bit of grass and weed from ten feet of the ground round the house - *"cheel"* it all away, and then smooth over, and level with the hand or a rammer all the surface of the ground that has been so cleared. Next cover this ground with the powdered brick bats called *"Soorkee"*. If you sprinkle the ground with water before and after laying the *soorkee* it will stick all the better. The next step will be the lawn.

A lawn, an absolute necessity

The shape and size of this will depend very much on how your carriage-drive lies. Most of the houses have a carriage-drive straight from the road to within a few yards of the front of the house, which there dividing forms itself into a semi-circular loop to the right, and to the left, uniting under the porch, or if there is no porch, at the front door. It is much too expensive to make a new carriage-drive, so, however it may go, we shall leave the drive alone and first attend to the circular, pear-shaped, oblong, or square bit of ground which it surrounds, just in front of the house. Most probably it has a high *mehndee* hedge, enclosing the inevitable "mali's" patch-work-garden. A crowding up of innumerable little patches of plants, with pathways nine inches wide, intersecting the arrangement with painful precision. Now, if you decide to let that eyesore remain where it is, then you need not trouble to read any more of this manual! Stay, we have already agreed to *improve* our outside surroundings, so there is no objection to taking away the mali's patch-work-garden; but, before we do this, let us see whether it is

A Suitable time of year for beginning a proper garden

From June to February is the best time for gardening. But March, April and May may be occupied in many little directions mentioned further on. We will consider that you have decided to begin your garden in June. If the front of your house *has* an enclosure like that described above, it must be cleared away. *It really must!* If you leave it as it is, the effect of whatever else you may do will be entirely spoiled. The beauty of the finest picture would be greatly marred if it were badly framed and badly hung; in the same way, the beautiful effect of your flowers will be lost if you don't place them where they can look their best. So, as it is a good time of year, let us clear away the ground in front, level it, and plant in with *doob* grass, in the way described further on. See what is best amongst the plants you are clearing away, and reserve them for other places, such as

Shrubberies and Side-Walks

As we are going to have a garden only on a small scale, and as I cannot in a small manual like this give you any diagram, you must decide for yourself where you are going to have your lawn (I have said a lawn is an absolute necessity!), then, on either side of your lawn, have a shrubbery for massing plants that grow from three to ten or fifteen feet high. When you have decided where you will have these, then, from the space you have cleared in front, transplant anything you think worth keeping. If there is a *mehndee* hedge encircling the mali's patch-work-garden, this hedge must be taken up and planted somewhere at the back of your house, or in any convenient spot that is well shaded and not conspicuous, because this is where you are to have your

Work-yard Enclosure

You must have this sort of shut-in place to do all your work of seed-sowing, transplanting, and general messing. Mixing of soils is very messy work; and broken flower-pots and withered leaves, which you will find most useful, must be stowed away in this workshop enclosure or *kar-khana.* If you have no *mehndee* hedge to clear away, some sort of thatch, just temporarily, will do, until you decide with what sort of hedge you will screen your *kar-khana.* Now let us go back to the space you have cleared. Stand at your front door and look at the ground spread just before you and imagine how nice it would be if you had an emerald green sward to rest your aching eyes upon; open, clear from all obstruction, so as to give you fresh sweet air to breathe. Then turn your eyes to the left and to the right and imagine beds and banks to sweet bright flowers, that "solace for humanity" as Ruskin calls them, and you will, I'm sure, be quire determined that such enjoyment *shall* be put within your own reach and that of your friends.

However large or small the immediate space just in front of your house may be, grass it over and have the carriage-drive sprinkled with red *soorkee,* as gravel in India is not procurable. If this is to be your only lawn, then let your shrubberies lie on the outer sides of your carriage-drive, leaving eight or nine feet of space all along between the carriage–drive and shrubbery for the massing and arrangement of flowers only. So if you stand on the grassy space in front of your house, the arrangement on each side will be, red carriage-drive, bordered all along with a flower-bed eight or nine feet wide, composed of flowers, and this flower-border banked up with a background of shrubs and foliage plants. Even this small extent of gardening will be a "joy for ever." As you read to the end of this manual you will see what you can have in bloom from one year's end to another. Let creepers twine round the pillars or posts of your porch, if you *have* a porch, but not so as to shut out the air or the view. Let flower-pots stand along the edge of your verandah, if you have a verandah, and along the nice ten feet of clearance, that first act of yours to "clean up" the outside of your house. There are no end of pretty creepers recommended to you, but these must not be trained anywhere on to your roof, or your walls, for three reasons : first, creepers on a house provide harbour for snakes (oh, horror!); second, creepers obstruct ventilation and harbour mosquitoes (again horror!); third, nothing makes a house look more untidy than draggled, unkept creepers. So, please, grow your pretty creepers where they will be a pleasure – not a pain.

Mali

The expense for keeping up this small garden will be five rupees a month to your *mali* for looking after and watering your flowers and shrubs. One extra rupee per month to your house *bhistie* for watering your grass-plot every evening, and eight annas per month extra to your grass-cutter for cutting your grass-plot once a week with the shears you will provide for him (*See* "Garden Tools"), and keeping your carriage–drive free from weeds. Any grass-cutter will be very glad of those extra monthly eight annas for doing a few minutes' work every day. Your *mali,* if he looks properly after your flowers and draws the water for watering them, will not have time for the work the bhistie and grass-cutter engage to do. If you have rather a large lot of plants, dispense with the *bhistie* and grass-cutter at Re. 1–8 and keep one of the *mali*'s many *"bhaies,"* a *chokra,* on Rs. 3 to help the *mali* all round. I do not venture to say a word about the culture of vegetables, but as I am anxious we should keep on good terms with the *mali,* let me advise you to allow him to grow a patch of vegetables on his own account near his hut. The produce of this little patch will realise just enough to compensate him for the disappointment he felt on being engaged to look after a flower garden pure and simple. *Malis* like to live well (like most persons!), so, though it is a foregone conclusion that your flowers will be stolen, and the deft fingers of the *mali*'s wife will weave them into garlands to sell to the devotees at the nearest temple, your *mali* will remain a discontented man and not take the care you expect him to take of your flowers, till you give him that vegetable patch for his *very own,* then all will go well. After making this small garden, if you think you will, in addition, venture on a large scale.

Garden on a larger scale

Say a lawn a little larger than a tennis-court, or suitable to hold a garden-party, also a "rosary," or rose-walks and conservatory like what you will find described later on, the expense will then increase by engaging more men, and may be taken to stand thus :- *mali* on Rs. 5 a month; three assistants for drawing water, &c., on Rs. 4 each; and one boy on Rs. 3; total Rs. 20. I take it for granted you have a well, or more than one, so your mali's three assistants will make the water-channels to suit all the purposes of watering, and (I hope you won't mind) you will have to make three reservoirs, one in the conservatory, one near your lawn, and one near your shrubbery that borders your carriage-drive. These reservoirs must be made thoroughly *pucca,* of bricks and cement, and so will last for many years. If your landlord is made to understand how much the value of his property will be enhanced and his ground improved by all you are doing in the way of gardening, he, most probably, will defray the cost of those reservoirs himself, since they will remain his property when you vacate his house. In any case, the outlay will be only a few rupees.

Preparing ground for the Lawn

Have your ground ploughed up, or thoroughly well dug up in the hot weather-May would be a good month. Let the clods lie open for a few days, to air the ground. Then have the clods broken into small pieces, and all the grass, weeds and roots picked out. Level it as perfectly as you can raking it over and over again. This will occupy several weeks, but as your men will not have anything particular to do in the garden in the hot weather, their attention can very well be devoted to the making of the lawn, which is to be the chief feature in your garden. Indeed if you can't make a garden, make *only a lawn,* or grass-plot, and this, with cleanly-kept *soorkee* paths and a few plants in the pots, will be sufficient to keep up the degree of harmony you intend to maintain between the outside and inside appearance of your abode. After there has been a good fall of rain, you will find your ground *settle,* and you will then be able to detect the inequalities of the surface and repair them. Rake over and remove all weeds not observed before.

Grass for your Lawn

Grass should be *doob* grass, which is procurable everywhere, at all events near stables. The grass-cutters bring *doob* for the horses, and as they always beat it to free the grass from the earth round the roots, the seeds of the *doob* fall with the earth, and germinate directly the rains begin. I can't in any other way account for the constant supply of *doob* grass to be found growing round about the stables. However, you will get it from any place most convenient. Have it dug up, roots and all, then have it chopped, *not shorter than three inches.* Bunches of it should be put together by one man and handed to another man to be chopped, bunch by bunch, into pieces *three inches long.* My reason for emphasizing the method of cutting is this,-if the cutter just clutches at a heap and chops away inch by inch, more than half the grass will be destroyed, and this will account for many bare patches appearing, even where the grass has been planted quite as thickly as any other part of the lawn. When your grass is all chopped up, then mix it into a paste of the proportions - two baskets of chopped grass, one basket of earth, one basket of cow–dung, one shovelful of wood ashes. Add as much water as will form it into a consistency thick enough to admit of its being spread on your ground like paste one inch thick. Your *mali* will call this process *leepna*. If it is not raining, water it with a watering-can. The next day roll it with a *bailan* on.

Stone-roller

This can be had at any quarry, and the size should be such as one man can pull easily, say, two feet long and one foot thick. A roller of this size, with its iron fixings, will cost you from Rs. 3 to Rs. 5, according to the distance of the quarry from whence it may be brought. As I am giving only my own experiences, and talking to you only about small gardens, you must not be surprised if I tell you that a lawn, about double the size of a tennis-court, is better if watered by the hand, than if it were flooded. So as soon as the rains are over, let your men water your lawn exactly as they water your plants, with a watering-can every evening. You can't have a lawn kept like velvet without a

Lawn-mower

This most necessary implement has for years been a crux in lawn-making, the price being prohibitive. Knowing this, I wrote to the Superintendent of the Canal Works at Roorkee on the subject of cheap lawn-mowers, and find he has lawn-mowers of three sizes, at the following prices :–

		Rs.
No. 1, 12 inches wide	... ...	40
No. 2, 16 inches wide	... ...	50
No. 3, 20 inches wide	... ...	70

This considerably improves the prospect of having a lawn in every little garden, for no one would mind paying Rs. 40 for a 12–inch lawn-mower. Then, again, I have seen advertised a 10–inch lawn-mower at about Rs. 24. So now no garden-lovers need sigh in vain for a lawn! Well, when you have got it, please see that the grass is cut twice or thrice a week in the rains, and at least once a week during the rest of the year. One little bit of advice I must give you here, insist on your *mali* cleaning the mower when he has done with it, and bringing it into your verandah where you can see for yourself that it *is clean* and where it will be safe from the mali's enterprising children, who can never resist the temptation of using it for their own playful purposes. To avoid ridges in the grass, have it mown first one way, then right across the other way, and immediately the mowing is done, have the lawn *swept up*. Never omit the sweeping up if you wish your grass to have a good colour. The day after mowing, the grass should be well rolled. Paley, writing about grasses, says : "They thrive under a treatment by which other plants are destroyed. *The more their leaves are consumed, the more their roots increase.*" The last sentence I have put in italics, because I want you to remember that the more like velvet you wish your lawn to appear, the more you must.

Mow, Sweep, Roll, Water

You may have heard of the American gentleman who was amazed at the wonderful beauty of the lawns of a certain College at Oxford, and enquired what was the secret of their treatment. "Oh, it has been cut and rolled, cut and rolled." The American expecting to have much more difficult processes disclosed towards the attainment of such perfection, said: "Yes, and then?" The reply was – "Oh! then just go on cutting and rolling for five hundred years, and you will see the result!"

Rosaries and Rose-walks

Where you have a shrubbery, reserve some space for a rosary, for roses that are climbers and ramblers, like Maréchal Niel, Gloire de Dijon, &c. (*See* "Roses"), look their best where they are not cramped. The dwarfs, or roses that do not grow very high, look best on either side of a walk, with twelve or eighteen inches of space reserved in front for annuals, and also a 6 or 7–inch border for grass. Along two sides of my lawn I had roses, annuals and grass planted in this manner, with a *soorkee*-coloured walk six feet wide running between, and the result was delightfully satisfactory. I hope you will have plenty of room, so that none of your walks should be *less* than six feet wide. They may be wider, but certainly not narrower. See that your roses get all the sunshine there is; roses that get only the morning or only the afternoon sun will not bloom perfectly. The same advice applies also to foliage shrubs and plants of bright colouring.

Treatment of Roses

For each rose-bush have a hole dug *at least* eighteen inches deep and eighteen inches wide, fill these holes with soil composed as follows : Two parts common earth, one part leaf-mould, one part old cow-dung (*gobur*) or sheep-dung (cow-dung is best).

Roses may be planted from 10th October to 10th November in the plains of India, and in the hill stations during the months of February and June. If they have travelled a long way, shield them after you have planted them from the mid-day sun only, for two or three days. When you see that they have recovered from their journey, snip off only the ends of their branches. It does not do to prune your newly-planted roses to the same extent as the roses that have been in your garden for years. Your old roses must be treated differently. In the plains change the soil from 10th October to 15th November, the earlier date for the southern parts and the later date for the northern parts of India. In the hills the transplanting is best done before the rains set in, and in the month of February mulching and manuring will give you a second crop of roses during the summer. Open out the roots, remove the old soil, and replace with fresh soil *at once.* I don't at all approve of exposing rose-roots for several days, for in my experience the results have been disastrous. I tried it in the Central Provinces and in the North-West Provinces, and lost most of my best roses in consequence.

After you have renewed the soil, and your roses have rested for three or four days, prune them well. At this season they must get water every day. In December you will find the buds begin to form, then mulch, that is, *stir up the surface of the soil* and give liquid cow-dung once a week, and continue doing this all the time they are in flower, which ought to be till the middle of March. Through the hot months you need to do anything but water them in the evening. (*See* "Flowers in the Hills")

Rose Cuttings

Of course you want a great many rose-bushes, and you don't wish to go to much expense about them. Well, choose cuttings of the roses you like best, twelve inches long, make holes as directed above, but to the soil of each hole add a good handful of powdered charchoal and one of sand; into the middle of each hole sink *four together* of your cuttings, and see that quite six inches of them are well beneath the soil, leaving six inches above. Over these clusters of cuttings, that have been planted in full sunshine, you must keep grass cones during the day only, until you see that their new leaves are all well out; then they need no further protection but to be watered. Cuttings, put down in October and November, in groups of four, in the manner described look quite decent shrubs the following year, and much time is saved by planting them in this way from the very beginning just where they are to remain. *Remember the grass cones during the day, else the cutings will wither.* The rest of your cuttings plant in your "reserve patch" Put these down in lines, each sort in its own line, four inches apart. Climbing roses need not be so much pruned as those which do not climb. (*See* "Roses")

Articles necessary for garden use

The lawn-mower and stone-roller I have already mentioned. you will require a pair of garden shears with blades nine inches long, in wooden handles, price Rs. 3. All your hedges will need constant trimming, your shrubs will need clipping, and this work can't be done except with the big shears mentioned. Then another most useful kind, a pair of garden spring shears, price Rs. 2. This you can make use of yourself, and if, as I suggested in paragraph "*mali,*" your grass-cutter is to cut your small grass-plot, this is the best shears he can use, and with this your grass borders must be clipped. For your own use have one large and one small English watering can, price Rs. 3 to Rs. 3 - 8. For the mali's use (*See* paragraph "Kerosine Tins").

Galvanized wire netting, 2-inch mesh, at 4 annas per square yard, is most useful, especially in stations where white-ants abound. Galvanized wire "for horticultural purposes" is sold at 4 annas per pound, and nails of all sizes 4 annas per pound, both *absolutely necessary.* Two things your *mali* will ask you for are a knife and a pair of scissors for pruning purposes. I have always found it best to let him suit himself with these from the bazaar.

Each of your men must have a *koorpee;* for yourself you will want a large and a small trowel and a fork, for you will see that I ask you to look after your ferns yourself. The leading iron-mongers sell all the above mentioned articles.

Then you will want some baskets, also twine and small wooden pegs and some chalk for marking.

The Many uses of Kerosine Tins

You will smile when you read this paragraph, but in the end you will allow satisfaction to take the place of amusement, for you know we are to do all our gardening in the most economical way.

Pails – Let a blacksmith take off the tops of six or eight tins, fix a band of hoop-iron round the edge of the tins, and then fix a handle of thick iron wire similar to the English galvanized pails.

Seed-boxes – Cut some of the tins longwise; as a kerosine tin is about ten inches in diameter, it will give you two seed-boxes five inches deep; this is only one and-a-half inches less in depth than the ordinary twine boxes generally used for sowing seed. Have the bottom of these tin seed-boxes perforated with four holes half-an-inch wide to admit of drainage. These tin boxes are much less likely to harbour insects and ants than wooden boxes. Have three or four of these tin seed-boxes perforated with holes a quarter of an inch square closely all over the bottom, to use sieves for sifting your soils and your powdered *soorkee.*

Watering cans – Cut off, diagonally, half the top of a tin, have an iron band put round the top similar to that put round the pails. At the open corner have a wire ring instead of a handle, at the closed corner have the spout fixed, at the top of the tin have a wire handle (like those on the pails) placed diagonally. When your pails and cans wear out, have the ironwork transferred to fresh tins. In this age we are nothing if not economical!

For putting away your different kinds of bulbs, have a few tins with lids to shut down.

Again, these tins may be cut and painted in many ways as *jardinieres* and *cache pots,* but one particularly good way is to remove the top of the tin and paint it all over with black japan (Re. 1 per bottle) which dries instantly, then on the four panels paint some simple design-grass butterfries, &c., &c., with Bessemer's gold paint (Re. 1 per bottle); this also dries at once.

As a stand for your black and gold tin, have a crate made exactly like four Oxford picture-frames joined to form a square. It may be made of any wood; at the four inside lower corners let there be small ledges to support the tin. Gild the frame with Bessemer's gold paint, and put your tin into it. Improve upon this idea for keeping pots in drawing-rooms, verandahs, &c., Odd pieces of tin will be required for your fern-boxes, &c. (*See* "Ferns")

Conservatory

Conservatory is a grand word, but by using in I don't mean to conjure up visions of expensive glass-houses, and frighten you out of the hope of having one. No, you can make a beautiful conservatory without a single pane of glass. If you are fortunate enough to have one, two, three, or half-a-dozen big, shady trees, such as mango, jaman, loquat, or any trees that retain their foliage all the year round, there you are already provided with the roof of your conservatory. If you have a great many trees to choose from, select a group within view of your lawn and easy of access. If I tell you about my own conservatory and how I made it, you will more easily understand how to set about making your own. Well, on the furthest side of my lawn I hapened to have one mango and four loquat trees, growing just so far from each other as to form a shade on an area of ground forty by thirty fet. Along the north and south side of these trees I put up screens of bamboo trellis, seven feet high and forty feet long, secured to poles driven into the ground at distances of six feet. To the east, facing the lawn, I left the entire side, thirty feet, quite open (*Note* - Ferns like early morning sun), so that from the lawn there was a pretty view of the interior of the conservatory. The west side, too, had the same height of trellis screen with an arched doorway. This arched doorway, though it faced the west, did not let in the afternon sun, beacuse fifteen feet away from the doorway was another trellis, which screened off the sun all the afternoon. These enclosures were made in May, and as soon as the rains began I planted ipomea and quisqualis (*See* I. and Q.) along the outer side of the trellis, and very soon it was entirely covered with green. Next came the making or rockeries and ferneries. These were in different forms against and around the trunks of the trees, all stereotyped regularity being avoided. In one corner of my conservatory, on the side nearest the well in the garden, I built a *pucca* reservoir, four and-a-half feet square, and three feet deep. To hide this reservoir from view, I built on the edge of two sides of it two feet of wall with a flat top. On the top I keep pots of all sort of pretty things, which are changed in their season, and against the wall, hiding it completely; is a fernery bordered with saxifrage and *pilea muscosa* (*see* S. and P.). In the other ferneries I have kerosine tins (which were first tarred inside and outside to preserve them from rust) sunk here and there and kept filled with water, so that the evaporation may increase the moisture for the plants. You will notice I make use of two words fernery and rockery. Of course rocks are used in the formation of both, but as mine is an open air sort of arrangement, in the ferneries I put nothing but ferns, and in the rockeries there are palms, lilies and foliage plants of sorts, some of them in pots sunk between the rocks, so that they can easily be changed in their seasons. Hanging baskets made of wood, wire, moss, &c., hang from the branches, and to make perches for hanging things on, some stout bamboos are placed across here and there neatly tied into the forks of the trees. The pretty-drooping grass (*See* "Grasses") clothes the trunks of the trees, while ivy, *pilea muscosa*, and saxifrage creep into all vacant spaces and thrive most comfortably. All the ground in this conservatory is raised a few inches above the level of the garden, so that water should not lodge here. It is kept scrupulously free from weeds, and an occasional renewal of the *soorkee* gravel makes it bright and clean. The plants here are all watered twice a day (except when it rains), morning and evening, with watering cans. This does not take long to do, as the water is close at hand in the reservoir. In the hot months the ground of this consevatory, as well as the plants, is watered twice a day. Rustic stands of different kinds, with pretty boxes of ferns, canes, &c., stand everywhere, leaving plenty of room to move about. I must tell you that the palms, canes, ferns and eucharis lilies remain in this place from one year's end to another. It is only such things as crotons, coleus, caladiums, &c., that are removed hence when they are at rest, or the weather is too frosty. The rocks or stones, of which these rockeries and ferneries are formed, are chiefly large and small lumps of brick refuse from kilns and of irregular blocks of *kunkur* from quarries. The brick refuse being porous, retains moisture, and *kunkur* is what ferns take to most kindly. The great knots of gnarled bark formed on trees by parasites, and called by the natives *bandha-ka-girrah*, form excellent receptacles for ferns, and white-ants do not find it palatable. In the rockeries I used leaf-mould. In the ferneries, soil prepared for ferns. (*See* "Ferns") For two years the bamboo screens round this conservatory stood very well, but at the end of that time, all the creepers collapsed owing to white-ants having completely destroyed the posts and all the bamboo trellis. However, at a very small expense, I built up brick pillars eighteen inches square and seven feet high, at distances of six feet; tarred poles were connected from pillar to pillar, quite on the top, and to these I nailed wire netting three feet wide. (*See* "Articles for garden use") The fallen creeperes were helped up to the netting with stout twine, and in a few days the screens were better than ever. This creeper-covered screen being only seven feet high, admits plenty of light and air from the top, but it keeps off all the *hot winds* of summer and the *cold winds* of winter, and experience has taught me that it is the *hot winds* more than anything else that destroys delicate things in the plains. In this open air conservatory, which has the partial shade of trees on the top and which is protected at the sides from the hot winds by that dense screen of creepers, the ferns in the trays and the ferneries remain from year's end to year's end *in all weathers* and thrive wonderfully. Indeed, I can honestly tell you that, even in their mounttain habitation they don't grow much better than they do here. The palms, canes, and foliage plants, too, all grow here happily and healthily in the brightest luxuriance, sheltered from that arch-fiend, the hot winds. Let me persuade you to make even a small conservatory on my most simple plan. The trees, of course, add much to the beauty of this arrangement, and make it appear almost like a glade in a natural forest. If you have no trees, don't despair. I too have been equally destitute, but took care of my ferns, &c., by making a shed twenty feet square, flat on the top, with a roof of coir-matting, which could be drawn aside like a photographer's curtain. This shed had creepers twining round the outer poles, and ten feet away from the shed were trellis screens such as I have already described; but these screens were placed rather zig-zag, so as to dodge the sun and give this conservatory rather a *mazy* appearance. However, the wind was kept out, and my dear plants lived very happily.

Garden Soils

Garden soils one of the very first things you must do when you begin gardening is to have a big hole dug by the side of your "work-yard enclosure." Make this hole ten or twelve feet square and six feet deep; the earth dug out of this hole carry over and store up in one corner of your workshop..Let all the dried leaves, weeds, grass, &c., cleaned up from your compound, be always thrown into this hole; impress it clearly on the memory of your cook's mate (*See* "Baker and Cook") that the couple of kerosine-tin pails kept in your kitchen for the purpose of collecting the solid refuse of the kitchen fireplace, - as the wood and charcoal ashes should be daily and regularly emptied, - the refuse into the leafpit, the ashes into your workshop, for you will want the ashes and bits of charcoal later on.

If the knight of the kitchen is fined once or twice for leaving refuse anywhere near your kitchen, he will become, oh! so smart in placing that refuse where you so particularly want it! Now you have plain earth, ashes and some leaf-mould getting ready. You want besides cow-dung (or sheep-dung), a small heap of sand, a good big heap of brickbats, and a heap of *kunkur.* This is not the place to maralize, and you may not be particularly interested in the well-being of your servants' children; but allow me to say that, as your brickbats have to be pounded up into *soorkee,* you will help those children to "earn an honest livelihood" if you set them to work and pay them a few coppers for pounding your *soorkee.* If you can possibly manage it, make a channel from the bath-rooms of your house to the leaf-pit. All the soap water utilized in this way and mixed up with your leaves and refuse will soon give you excellent leafmould. If the contents of the pit can be so watered and tossed about in the damp with a pole, your leaf-mould will be ready to use in six months; if not, you must wait for the rains to rot it, which it will do in two years. But if you want to plant your garden out at once, you can buy this leaf-mould *(puth-thee-ke-kâth)* from some native gardener your *mali* is sure to find for you, if you make it worth his while. Always sift your soils before mixing. If your cow and sheep-dung can be *partially* burnt before using, so much the better, as it ought not to be used fresh except for surface-dressing where recommended, later on.

Seed Sowing

For all your seeds of annuals use the following mixture of soil: two parts leaf-mould, one part plain earth, and one part composed of half-burnt cow-dug and powdered charcoal. Mix these four parts together, and sift again. (*See* "Garden Soils".) If you ar going to use the seed-boxes of kerosine tins, put a flat crock over each hole at the bottom : if you use wine cases, place two inches of crocks all over the bottom. Fill up your seed-boxes with the prepared soil to within an inch of the top, water gently to enable it to settle; when settled, sprinkle lightly with a little dry soil, and with your finger draw lines half-an-inch deep and three inches apart, and into the furrows made by your finger drop your seeds, and over them sprinkle quite half-an-inch or more of soil, and then smooth over the entire surface of your box with the palm of your hand lightly. It is much the best plan to sow seeds in lines, leaving vacant spaces between, because when the seeds germinate and the seedlings are big enough to be transplanted, you can stick in your fork or trowel without breaking the tender roots, as you most certainly would, were the seeds sown promiscuously all over the box. Water you seeds the day after they are sown very gently with a *fine rose* to your watering can, continue to water every evening; keep your boxes where they will get only the very least sun, say, for one hour only in the early morning, but give them all the *light* you can; the north side of a good thick hedge would be the best place for your boxes. If it rains, as it sometimes does even at the end of October, bring your boxes into the verandahs, or cover carefully with boards, else your seeds will be all washed away! As your seedlings grow bigger, give a little more sunshine. When they are transplanted into pots and into the ground where they are to remain, protect them from the sun for a day or two, and when fully established, let them have all the sunlight possible. You can save seeds of some things, and you can get acclimatised seeds from your nearest public gardens. For English seeds, send to Sutton & Sons, Reading, England, as their seeds can always be depended on.

Flower-Pots

When you have read through this little manual and noted what you wish to have growing in pots, you will be able to form an idea of how many pots you will be likely to require and the different sizes. One thing you must remember, *the potter can't make pots during the rains, so you must lay in your stock beforehand.* You will want them from five to twelve inches in diameter: the 5-inch pots are very nice for small ferns and single specimens of annuals, such as pansies, asters, &c., 8-inch pots are suitable for oxalis, balsams, & c., 10 and 12-inch pots for lilies, plams, canes, &c., and such things as you wish to bring inside your rooms. Such shrubs as roses should not have pots less than 18 inches in diameter. When lilies and caladiums, &c., are taken out of pots, keep the empty pots carefully piled upside down at one side of your work-yard. Always wash an old pot before using again. It will save trouble to order your potter to make holes for drainage at the bottom, when he is moulding the pots; if not, a good many of the pots will be cracked when the *mali* comes to drill the holes. According to the size of your pots, you must fill the bottom with crocks from one to three inches, before you fill up with soil, to prevent the earth from being waterlogged. *Hirmajee* is the native name of the red earth that gives the pots such a bright, rich colour. If you don't mind the expense, a little kerosine oil mixed with the earth is better than water, because when the pots are painted with it, grubs and ants are less likely to creep up. The smell is objectionable, but it soon passes off. A few saucer-like gumlas, *pir-ritch,* for standing lilies, &c., in water, must be procured, also some with holes in the bottom for planting your violets, achimenes, &c.

Gardening Books

These are without number, all valuable for the different kinds of information given to different kinds of gardeners, and when you and I, who are only *beginners* in the art, have mastered the rudiments and want to increase our knowledge, we must get some of these delightful books. Firminger for Bengal and North-West Provinces; Woodrow for Western India and Madras; these are two most comprehensive books. Then there are others less expensive, such as "Practical Gardening for Indian Amateurs," by R. Barton West; "Amateur Gardener in the Hills;" "The Indian Amateur Gardener," by Landolicus; another very useful little book "Indian Vegetable Garden," by W. Gollan, Superintendent, Botancial Gardens, Saharanpur, tells you a good deal about the cultivation of flowers also, and I can't say how many more. Then there is Colonel Beddome's Book on "Ferns," and Annie Pratt's "Ferns of Great Britain,' will teach you, in the most charming manner, an immense deal about all kinds of ferns. But by-and-bye, when you have learned the simple "A.B.C." you are attempting now, you must reward yourself with a treat, which is the possession of W. Robinson's "English Flower Garden." In his Preface he says:– "Few know the many flowers fitted to adorn our open air gardens. Without such knowledge progress is not easy. It is useless to discuss systems of arrangement if the beauty of the flowers is sealed to us." So Mr. Robinson, in his fascinating book, gives us more than three hundred pages of illustrations, from which we can learn to distinguish by sight more than eighteen hundred different kinds of plants. On the subject of flowers, it is the most instructive book in the world in English. Another book which is intensely interesting, and which you ought to read, is 'The Language of Flowers," published by Messrs. Saunders and Otley, Brook Street, Hanover Square.

Then another little book you must not go without is *your own note-book!* When you go into your garden in the morning, take this little book with you as a matter of course, as you would take your gloves or your sun hat! Opposite the date, pencil all you do, and leave a margin for additional remarks as you gain experience. You should enter what plants are bought and at what time, &c.

The mali trembles when he sees
you making notes about your trees;
And should your note-book disappear,
He'll steal your plants without a fear!

All I have told you in this little book is gathered from notes made in my garden for seventeen years.

Garden Stands

Garden stands of different kinds can be very easily made under your own direction; those of gnarled wood are most rustic and suitable. Buy, in the first instance, one or two cart-loads of firewood, just as it is brought in from the jungles: I mean before the firewood vendors cut it up into billets. In any carpenter's workshop you are sure to find some "prentice" boys; hire a smart lad on 5 or 6 annas a day, and set him to work at your "thi-paies," the one word by which they express *stands* of sorts. With soft wire, make *small* models of the sort of stands you want, and then set the lad to work to cut and nail the pieces of crooked wood together. Let us imagine a skeleton table without a top - four legs three feet high, held into a square shape with transverse bars at the top and at the bottom, the length of the bottom bars two feet, and of the top bars one foot, this will form a skeleton table, broad at the base and narrow at the top. Diagonally across the four *sides* of this table let the boy-carpenter nail a rough, irregular lattice-work of the thinnest and most crooked pieces of your firewood, and there you have a delightful rustic stand! Let him go on and make others in the same way, varying the shapes sometimes by producing *three*-legged, triabgular stands, and six-legged round stands, and so on, your own ingenuity furnishing other wire models for his guidance. The Jail at Shahjehanpur makes these rustic stands at eight annas each of various sizes, "nested" to occupy less space in transport by rail. You might get one from there to give your lad a clearer idea of what you want him to do.

But you have not done with your carpenter-boy yet! The wooden cases in which your kerosine tins come can be cut up into.

Trays, Hanging Baskets, &c.

All odds and ends of deal boxes, too, can be utilized for this purpose. Let the boy saw them into strips half-an-inch wide, and cut these strips into lengths of 6, 10, or 12 inches. He will do several hundreds in a day, and you will not have too many. All these pieces ought to have a hole bored through them within an inch of each end. The 6-inch pieces to be strung with wire for hanging baskets, and the 10 and 12-inch ones to be strung in the same way for the trays, and formed into six, eight, or ten-cornered receptacles, according to your requirements. These nests or receptacles need not be more than five or six strips deep, and your tinman must fit them with tin bottoms, and see that the pieces cut for these bottoms are large enough to have half-an-inch turned up all round. The horticultural wire should be laced underneath the tin so as to support the weight of soil, *kunkur*, &c., which are to be put into it. The boy may cut boards to fit the bottom of the nests if you prefer it, and the tin lining may rest on these boards instead of on the wire lacing. I prefer the wire lacing, as the boards are apt to swell and warp.

The pieces of wire used for stringing the strips together should be twisted off into a loop; you will fix your suspending wires into these loops when you come to hang up your baskets.

Each kerosine tin has a ring of strong iron wire by which it is lifted. Tell your tinman to bend these into hooks in the form of an open S, for you will find them most useful for all the nests, baskets, and pots you wish to suspend with wire.

Pillar Stands

Pillar stands roughly made of bricks I find very useful and convenient. Place three bricks flat on the ground, letting the corners touch each other, so as to leave a triangular space in the middle; place three more bricks on the first three, letting each brick *lie across the corners of the lower ones.* Pile them in this three-cornered style till you have a pillar from 24 to 30 inches high. The outside will present a honeycomb appearance, and in the little triangular cells you can plant small ferns, like "maiden-hair," or *lunulatum, caudatum,* &c. The centre of the pillar fill up with earth, and on the top place a tray or pot of ferns, &c. These pillars keep damp a long time, and are really very nice for conservatories. If not required after a certain time, they can easily be removed.

Cyanotis ("Wandering Jew") trained up these pillars will take root and clothe them very prettily; of course you can make these pillars of a larger circumference than three bricks, but you will find an odd number, 5, 7, and so on, gives a prettier appearance than if made with an even number.

We shall now proceed to consider our plants in alphbetical order.

Acalyphas

Acalyphas are handsome foliage shrubs, suitable for shrubberies and for pots in verandahs, the cultivation of them gives no trouble. The rainy season is the time that these plants are in their glory. Begin with two kinds, *Acalypha Wilkesiana tricolor,* and *Acalypha obovata.* Get cuttings a foot long, and plant them first in the shade, and when you see new leaves have sprouted, take them up and plant them where they are to remain. In the winter those in the ground will shed their leaves, and should then be pruned to within two or three feet of their base. Those in pots, if kept in verandahs, will not shed their leaves but change colour somewhat; prune these just before the rains begin. When the monsoon has well set in, put out those in pots to get as much rain as they can. At this time all your acalyphas will send out new shoots vigorously, and the beauty of their rich, glowing shades of red and brown will reward you well for the little trouble you have taken with them. Tubs of it, in porches where they can be seen against the sunlight, make gorgeous show. Watering *over* the leaves suits best.

Achimenes

Achimenes are small plants with exquisitely beautiful flowers, and must be grown in hanging baskets, in trays supported on stands, or in pots kept on good thick bricks. Send to the nearest Government gardens for two kinds to start with : *Achimene Longiflora Major,* a pale, mauve, satin-like flower; and *Ambroise Verschaffelt,* flowers French grey. The are small tubers and are sold at a few annas per dozen. They increase three-fold each year, so a few dozens to start with will be sufficient. They do not require any *depth* of soil. Use the soil recommended for *seed-sowing,* adding a little more sand. Use the flat pots called *pir-ritch,* spread first a layer of dry grass, then a few small crocks, next fill up with soil - water the soil - make five holes with your finger about half-an-inch in depth, put one tuber in each, cover over each hole lightly, keep these saucer-pots on the edge of your verandahs where they will get plenty of light and air; *sun and rain spoil them.* For hanging up - here is a good way. Cut a square foot of your wire netting, spread it with moss, putting the pile or surface side of the moss next the wire, then a layer of coir or dried hay, spread over an inch of soil, sprinkle with water, plant five or six tubers, cover over with soil, make a ball by rolling up three or four crocks with moss, put this ball on the centre, then gently gather up the four corners of the wire netting and compress the whole into a round mass; suspend by wire and keep as moist as possible. When the flowers all die down, as they do when the rains are over, hang up these balls in a shed, or to a rafter in a godown. Next May - about the end - bring them out and sprinkle slightly with water, you will find shoots thrusting themselves out in all directions, and when the rain has fairly set in, these will form lovely globes of blossom. If you want to use the pots and saucers again, in which your achimenes are, stop watering when they die down, and when the soil is all but dry, turn out and carefully pick up the tubers, putting them away in dry sand till next May. Those in the round wire baskets are best left alone for two or three years, or till you think the moss wants renewing.

Sutton & Sons' tubers are the best. Where you wish to be economical, it is always advisable to start with the *best* in seeds, bulbs, &c.

Alternanthera amabilis

Alternanthera amabilis is the pretty variegated green and red and brown leaf edging so necessary for borders to flower-beds which you wish to have well defined and kept trim and tidy. It grows very quickly; you can probably get it for the asking from friends' gardens, or buy a few basketsful from the nearest public garden. Plant at the beginning of the rains as follows:- Cut it all up into pieces four or five inches long, and plant these pieces three together, in a line, leaving a space of two inches between the groups. This is the most economical arrangement, but, if you have plenty and to spare, you may plant two or three lines of it for each border, for the thicker it is the better. In the rains, when it grows very fast, keep it trimmed with your grass shears, planting all you clip off in a corner of your reserve plot, to draw upon for future need. In the hot weather, if it looks shabby, watering will set it all right again.

Amaranthus

There are different kinds of these charming foliage plants; get seeds of *Amaranthus tricolor and Amaranthus salicifolius;* sow sparsely on leaf-mould; take up the plants carefully when two or three inches high, and then plant out in bright sunshine. After the rains begin is the best time. They are pretty in clumps with a border of balsams, or by themselves, some should be put singly into 10-inch pots. These two kinds droop away in the very cold weather, but there is another kind, *Amaranthus melancholicus ruber*, which lasts all the year round. It grows from both seed and cutting; cuttings are best, as they take very readily. Put ten or twelve cuttings in to boxes in the rains, and keep these boxes on stands, as the branches droop over very prettily. At the end of the rains bring these stands into the verandahs where they will get the morning sun, or keep them under the trees in your conservatory. In December and January the plume-like sprays of flowers come out and are very useful for decorations. (*See* "Hints") Increase by plentiful cuttings put down anywhere, where they will be sheltered from frost. Amaranthus means *immortalilty,* (7th August,) and is devoted to St. Cajetan, 1547 A.D.

Asters

Asters have much to recommend them. They are easy of culture, make a lovely show, and the blooms, whether left on the plants or cut for decoration, last twice as long as other ordinary flowers. Sutton's varieties are splendid and never fail. Send for any or all of the following: "Mixture of delicate shades," "Mixed Victorias," "Mixed Comet," &c. Sow in October in boxes, dropping seed by seed in lines. When four leaves have developed, plant singly in 6-inch pots, keep in shade for four or five days, then place the pots in open sushine. Water at the root; save the seed.

Aristolochia

Aristolochia is a climbing shurb recommended for many reasons, its flowers are extremely curious, it grows easily from layers, is of rapid growth, has foliage thick and ever green, is very well adapted for twining round poles in conservatories or round pillars of porches, and its leaves, which are something like kidney-shaped ivy leaves, keep fresh for a long time after they are plucked, and are therefore most useful in foliage decorations. There are many kinds of *Aristolochia:* to begin with, ask for those with thickest foliage; plant in the rains.

Arundo donax

Arundo donax a tall, striped white and green grass, very effective if grown here and there in clumps of foliage plants in shrubberies, in rockeries with *Canna* and *Acalypha*. Get roots of it in the rains, and plant where it will get plenty of sunshine, but not where it will be subject to the force of the hot winds, which it does not like. It is very hardy when it once establishes itself, and grow all the better for being thinned of the side shots, which you may detach and plant elsewhere If any of these handsome reeds should appear to be fading away, water freely; if that does not revive it, leave it alone, you will find new plants sprouting in the rains the following season. Its flowering spikes should be preserved for decorations.

Arundo donax versicolor

Arundo donax versicolor is a dwarf kind of the same reed. Grow it in borders in your open-air conservatories, and in small pots to use in trays and for in-door decoration. Increase by removing the suckers during the rains. If your part of India is frosty, these pretty grasses will die down in winter; then you must cover up the pots with dry grass and leaves; when the rains begin they will all sprout again. (*see* "Hints")

Balsams

No garden should be without these most showy plants. If your garden is not very large, half an ounce of seed will be sufficient for you to start with. Get *best double mixed* varieties from Sutton & Sons.

Have a succession of sowings in August, September and October. Balsams want a lot of space. When sowing, drop each seed separately, so that the seedlings may not crowd too closely. As soon as four leaves have developed on each plant, take them up, and plant again in pots, making holes deep enough to receive the whole of the stem, so that the lower leaves may rest on the surface of the soil. As soon as they show a few more leaves, take them up again, and plant them in borders eight inches apart, or singly in pots, again taking care to sink them up to the lower leaves. Put a good many in pots, as they make a delightful show in-doors and in verandahs. As the plants throw out *side branches,* snip them off carefully, so that all the flowers should be borne on the centre stem only, to form quite a torch of bloom. Heavy rain spoils the flowers, so bring the pots under shelter if rain is continuous. Save the seed for the following year. Balsam means *impatience,* and is devoted to St. Lawrence Martyr, 258 – (10th August).

Bamboos

Bamboos are magnificently graceful! In a garden such as you and I are undertaking very few will be wanted. One by itself on a grass-plot, one or two here and there in the bare parts of your compound are greatly to be desired. Nothing can exceed the grace of the common bamboo – the vigorous kind – procurable everywhere.

There is a dwarf kind which you should grow in the centre of small grass-plots. Write to your nearest public garden for some *Bamnusa Nana,* they will increase largely each year, and you can multiply them by dividing the roots in the rains.

Mix a little sand with the ordinary garden soil and give your bamboos plenty of room to expand. When first planted water plentifully, after that only occasionally in the hot weather. Always cut away those stems that are fully developed and show scant leaves; the fuller, greener shoots will grow all the better. In a small garden, the single bamboos grown on grass-plots need not be allowed to grow higher than ten or twelve feet. Those at a distance in your compound may grow as tall as they like; but if you want it to add to the beauty of the view, you must cut away the old stems and prevent them spreading into a jungle. Plant and transplant in the rains. If large full-grown bamboos are to be transplanted, see that you dig well down, so as to take up with it plenty of the soil in which the roots are embedded.

Bauhinia – Kuchnar

This is more a tree than a shrub, but it is a lovely thing to have here and there in your compound, for, when in bloom in the hot months, its elegant azalea-like flowers will provide you with abundant decorations. (*See* "Hints") It can be propagated easily by seed sown at the beginning of the rains. Decide where they would look best, then have holes dug about three feet deep and in the middle of these place four or five seeds. Protect the holes with some brambles to prevent cattle going over them. It should be watered occasionally during its first hot season and may then be left to itself. *B. variegata* bears lovely blossoms of a peach-like mauve, blended with purple : *B. candida* has white flowers which are exquisite! I would like to see in every station an entire avenue of these trees as at Bareilly, and when in bloom, I can imagine nothing more beautiful or more fragrant.

Beaumontia grandiflora

I am sorry I can't give you any but the Latin name for this noble climber. You may have seen its grand branches of white lily-like flowers, and have naturally wished to have some for yourself. It can be grown from cuttings or seeds put down in the rains, and later on; but a better plan will be for you to buy a plant from the nearest Government garden, and when it is well established, make cuttings yourself. On an archway of brick, stone, or very strong poles, to mark entrance from one part of the garden to another, this magnificent climber is a sight worth taking some trouble about.

Bignonia

Beautiful, flowering creepers, blooming chiefly in the hot weather, or, more properly speaking, from February onwards. *Bignonia gracilis,* with pale lemon-coloured flowers, comes into bloom at the end of the rains in some places, Shahjehanpur for instance. *B. incarnata* has flowers shaded lilac and purple; *B. venusta,* most brilliant orange. these are all easily propagated by cuttings or layers in the rains and cold weather. *B. incarnata* and *B. venusta* are very vigorous and want strong support. *B. gracilis* is not so irrepressible. I don't approve of verandahs being blocked up with creepers, and though I admit that a thatched roof covered with *Bignonia venusta* is a really glorious sight, I prefer to train it on screens to hide the veiw of servants' houses, on an ugly bit of outhouse wall, on old, almost leafless trees, &c. All these bignonias are better for having the lower stems clipped after flowering.

Bombax malabaricum

Bombax malabaricum is a large, indigenous tree, generally found somewhere in the compound of most houses, and known as the 'silk cotton tree.' If you have any, leave them where they are, as they don't bear transplanting, and their shaded, deep red velvety flowers don't clash with other colours, as the raw magenta of the Bougainvillea does. If your compound will admit of it, plant some seeds of this in June, in the way recommended for *Kuchnar;* but let me advise you to plant this beautiful flowering tree in one or two large clumps, the holes for the seeds being dug fifteen feet apart. The flowers which appear in the hot weather are very effective for decorations. (*See* "Hints") I hope you won't be impatient at my advising you to plant things you might not reap the benefit of yourself, but remember our generous motto – "*See vos non vobis* – So you do not labour for yourselves!"

Bougainvillea

Bougainvillea introduced into Europe by De Bougainville, the French navigator, will be found in almost every garden laid out by a *mali.* If you have got it, don't keep it in your front garden, for its magenta-coloured bloom kills by contrast the effect of all the other flowers in your garden. Transplant it at the end of January to some distance from your house, near your outer gate or to hide servants' quarters, where, 'alone in its glory,' it will brighten up its surroundings. You must see this done yourself, for it is dear to the eyes of the *mali,* who will not banish it willingly, an unwillingness we must not be surprised at, for in an old French book– on the subject of flowers, on which Messrs. Saunders and Otley founed their charming "Language of Flowers" (and which I have advised you to read), there is a story told of how – "De Bougainville's South Sea Islander, on being taken to the Botanic gardens in Paris, knelt before this Otaheitan shrub, and kissed it as fondly as he would have kissed the lips of a beloved mistress."

There is a terra-cotta coloured variety of Bougainvillea that is well-worth growing.

Box (Sumatra Box)

Box *(Murraya Exotica and Sumatrana)*, native name is *Káminee.* Most desirable shrubs to have in your garden, both for their fragrant, bridal-looking flowers and their dark shining foliage. Get cuttings in the rains, and put them in your shrubberies or in the centre of small beds cut out in grass-plots. As the Sumatra Box is an evergreen, you may plant round it the following: – hot weather, amaryllis; – rains, coleus, balsams, &c.; – winter, coreopsis, bordered with white candy-tuft, or marguerites bordered with dark-coloured nasturtiums. As your shrubs grow big and strong, prune the lower stems in the rains, and plant them in your reserve plot for future use. You can't have *too* much of it.

Caladiums

Caladiums are handsome foliage plants you know very well, and which are grown from bulbs. To begin with, write in the hot weather for some of the inexpensive kinds. They will make a fine show in the rains, and when you have learned how to treat them properly, you can venture on other varieties. I don't know why caladium bulbs should be dear, when they are very easily grown and increase and multiply tremendously. In gardners' phraseology, caladiums begin to *"move"* in the hot weather. Put your smaller bulbs into 10-inch pots and the larger ones in 12-inch pots *in May, but don't water them!* If you do, they will outgrow their strength and look limp and 'leggy' just when they ought to look their best. When the rains begin, they will get on splendidly, and you can then water them freely. Plant them in the soil recommended for seed sowing, adding a little powdered charcoal, and when you see they have put out some leaves fully, you must begin to give them liquid cow-dung once a week, or every ten days. When you plant the bulbs in May, keep the pots in verandahs, or under a shady hedge where they can be protected from the sun and hot winds. Once they have started, arrange the pots where you will probably allow them to remain, because they like to settle themselves *towards the light*, and the light side of their position will be the *showy* side of the caladiums. Sink some pots in your rockeries, for your stands use the trays mentioned in paragraph "Trays." These should be kept in your conservatory in places where they will get plenty of light from the *top*. In this way they will make an *all-round show*, different from the one-sided show their humbler brohers in low pots will make. Caladiums grown high, grow better than those grown low. Those you will want for your fireplace, should be grown in boxes; you will find wine or kerosine cases filled with bulbs of different kinds the best for this pupose. One dozen bulbs to a case will be sufficient for a grand display. As the rains cease caladiums begin to droop: water them at this time only occasionally, and stop watering altogether when there are no leaves standing upright. If you require the pots for your chrysanthemums (which will want re-potting at this time) turn out your caladiums from the pots, but leave them as they are in their own soil for a day or two, to dry a bit. Then pick out the bulbs, and keep them in kerosine tins with plenty of dry sand or earth between the layers of bulbs. Keep the different kinds separately, so that you may know which is which the following May. If you can afford to let the caladiums remain in their pots, leave them standing in the sun for a month; then pile them one on top of the other in some safe place in your verandahs or godown, but beware of white-ants and rats! Beware also of the thieving malis who have spotted your best ones, and will quietly abstract the bulbs and tell you they rotted away. But strange to say, the rotted away caladiums will bloom the following year in the verandahs of some other house.

Camphire (Mehndee)

Camphire is one of the commonest yet most delightful of Indian shrubs. Solomon, in the 14th verse of the 1st chapter of his Song, says – "My beloved is unto me as a cluster of camphire in the vineyards of Engedi." In the original of this Song, written about 1,000 years B.C., the word translated 'camphire' is *copherius,* the Egyptian equivalent of which is *hennah,* called in India *mehndee.* In a most interesting lecture on "Camphire and Camphor," by J.C. Sawyer, F.L.S., in the *Scientific American* of 30th April, 1892, you will find all sorts of information about those two things; but I shall here quote just a little about camphire only. This camphire, or *hennah,* is Pliny's "Cypres of Egypt," and the women of Egypt and other Eastern countries stain not only the palms of their hands and the soles of their feet with a paste of *hennah* leaves, but also the tips of the fingers, the nails and the knuckles, from which custom probably arises the designation of Aurora as "rosy" or "rosy-fingered." The word "cluster" found in the text refers to the flowers of this plant which are of a golden yellow, are borne in clusters and are remarkably fragrant. It is known to the Arabs as *hennealhennah,* has been cultivated from the earliest times, and is common throughout India, Kabul and Persia, as well as along the caost of the Mediterranean. Botanically it is known to us as the *Lawsonia inermis* of Linnaeus. It has been introduced in the West Indies, and is there known as *"Jamaica mignonette."*

Yes, the common *mehndee* of India is a shrub you ought to treasure. Nothing grows so fast in the way of hedging as this "tree mignonette." Nothing scents your garden so sweetly and delicately as its clustering blossoms, the pretty form and colour of which are something between myrtle blossoms and mignonette. Myrtle takes a long time to grow, and mignonette lasts only a few months, but the camphire of Solomon is with you always. As soon as the rains begin to fall, put down cuttings 18-inch long in ordinary soil; it will take root and grow at once. When wanted for a fence, put down three or four rows of the cuttings in a foot wide furrow, and let it grow to a height of four feet. The top should be cut very evenly several times during the rains with your big garden shears and clipped along the sides so as to make the hedge from the top to bottom of one uniform width. Let me impress upon you the importance of keeping your hedges well and neatly trimmed, for however nice your lawn and beds may be kept, an untidy hedge will spoil the effect in the same way as a battered and broken frame would detract from the look of a picture.

Besides your *mehndee* in the hedge, let me advise a number of clumps of it to be grown as flowering shrubs: you will want all the flowers. The hedge being constantly clipped will not be able to put forth its blooms; but those on the clumps should be allowed to grow to its utmost height, and need only to be slightly trimmed so as to keep it in rather an oval form. Oh! this *mehndee* is a most lovely thing, and I am much surprised that its beauty is not more appreciated. (*See* "Hints")

Candy-tuft

Candy-tuft a profusely flowering, pretty, low-growing annual: good wide borders of the white kind next to other *bright* coloured annuals, look very effective, especially if you will keep a perfect outline by pinning in stray stems with long pins made like huge hair-pins out of your "horticultural" wire. Small diamond-shaped beds of white candy, with a centre and a narrow border of dark red phlox, are extremely pretty. Decide where you will keep it, because (as it won't bear transplanting) you must sow it where it is to remain. Put some in 5- and 8-inch pots, as you will find it a great addition to any mass of pretty flowers you may wish to put together for in-door temporary decoration. Sow in October in the soil recommended for annuals. I don't advise purple candy-tuft, as you will have plenty of other purple and mauve in your small garden.

Canes

Canes are well worth cultivating, for their graceful shining foliage makes them ecxceedingly ornamental for both out-door and in-door purposes. If you are staying not far from swampy places where canes abound, you can easily procure clumps of them; if not, they do not cost much to buy at Government gardens; and if you treat them properly they increase and multiply very satisfactorily. Procure them when the rains have set in. With me they have always thriven splendidly in the following soil: One part ordinary earth, one part leaf-mould, one part sand, one part pounded *kunkur. Pray don't give them any manure.* The will like living in your rockeries, especially if these are placed against trees, as described in "Conservatories:" for then they will grow up right into the trees. Have as many as you can in 12-inch pots, planted singly, for in-door decoration, and keep these pots in any part of your conservatory where they will get plenty of light, but no sun directly on them. They don't like sun, and the beautiful *gloss* which is natural to them is lost in sunlight. Water at the root, and also all over. In the hot weather give them water twice a day if you can. In the winter shelter them from frost. The year after they are planted you may increase them if you see new shoots all round the pot. As they are frightfully thorny, the best way to set about this is to fold sacking, or a *Kummul* (horse blanket) round the cane, and tie loosely so as not to bruise the leaves. Dig round the roots, and cut away with a sharp knife those side shoots which you see have thrown out roots for themselves. Don't do this at any time but in the rains, and *at once* plant those you have separated. If you see any of the tall old stem turning yellow, cut them away: the new ones will grow all the better for it. Though canes like swampy places in the jungles, don't attempt to stand your pot canes in water ; they will all spot yellow and rot away if you do. Change your drawing-room canes every day, and don't keep them shut up at night. (*See* "Palms")

During the monsoon keep them where they will get as much rain as possible, as this is their growing time.

Canna

You will have known under the name of "shot-lily," their seeds being like shot. No large foliage plant grows more easily than canna. There is scarcely a garden where you don't find the common kind, *canna indica,* with broad green leaves and bright scarlet flowers. Plant some of this by your well, where it will grow in wanton wildness, and provide you with endless material for in-door decoration. The most handsome canna, and quite as easily grown as that just mentioned, has, unluckily, a frightful name–*C.! Warczewiczii*! This Russian gentleman has beautiful bronze-red or brown leaves, and very rich red flowers. Find room in your shrubberies for some of this kind, and for bringing in-doors grow some in kerosine tins, and let the tins stand in water. The roots are so quick-growing and strong, they would burst the pots! Where it is very cold, the canna will die down in winter. You may leave the roots where they are, or take them up and keep like caladium bulbs. These canna need no care; they come up and die down in their proper seasons. The one thing necessary for you to do is, to take them up and plant them in regular order.

Well-kept clumps of *C.Warczewiczii* on the borders of a green lawn look exceedingly well. If you grow canna from seed, sow seed in a pot, and keep the pot standing in water till the seed germinates. (*See* "Hints".)

Chrysanthemums

Chrysanthemums are lovely flowers that reward all the care taken of them. I do not in the least wonder that the Japanese, keen lovers of the beautiful in nature and art, should hold these flowers in reverence, and introduce them so constantly in all their designs. Thanks to the Superintendent of the Government Botanical Gardens at Saharunpur, nearly four hundred different kinds of chrysanthemums are now within reach of all amateur gardeners. Send to Saharunpur for a list and make your choice *before* February. From 15th February to 15th April they are available at two annas each! Try to have yours put down by *15th March* into soil composed of two parts leaf-mould and one part cow- or sheep-dung, to which add a sprinkling of sand and powdered charcoal. The sand and charcoal are to prevent the soil from clogging. Chrysanthemums hate sticky soil; and when you see any plant looking yellow and sickly during the flowering season, from October to March, turn it out, and put it into fresh soil with a little extra charcoal. When buds form, as they do about the beginning of October, snip away with fine-pointed scissors, at least half of what you see at the end of each stem : your flowers will be all the finer in consequence. When the buds swell they become very heavy, and the weight increases as the flowers expand and retain the dew, so you must support the stems by tying them to thin bamboo stakes. The stems are brittle, and if tied with twine, are easily cut. A good plan is to steep a yard or two of thin cottton cloth in green dye made by pounded leaves (mango, jamun, &c.), then tear the cloth into narrow strips and use for chrysanthemums. While the chrysanthemums are in bud and flower, give liquid manure once a week. There is one thing you must remember about these plants, and that is, you must transplant them *twice a year* – at the beginning of October before they flower, and at the end of February when they have done flowering. When their flowers are over, cut off those stems and plant them in a shady place on slightly raised ground. Most of these cuttings will take root and may be transplanted in October. See that they are watered in the hot weather, and during the rains you must take care they don't get water-logged, or else they will rot away. Chrysanthemums make a tremendous quantity of suckers, so in March and October take them up, shake away all the old soil, and separate the suckers, planting each separately. I advise you to have as many as you possibly can in *pots* of the 10 and 12-inch size, because you can move them where you want your best show of flowers, and, what is more important, move them out of the driving wind and rains. After the March transplanting, I keep all my pots on the two lower edges of my east verandah (*See* "Verandahs"); here they get all the morning sun, they are here sheltered from the hot winds of May and from excessive rain in the monsoons as they eaves of the verandah just prevent their being drowned. In this way I never lose a plant, not even a single branch! In the hot weather they should be watered all over the leaves plentifully with a watering-can. While they are in flower water at the root only. These lovely flowers come into bloom just before the roses, and make an almost startling show of colour. As they are inexpensive, most prolific, and not difficult to rear, I strongly recommend you to undertake their culture. (*See* "Hints") Chrysanthemum is the flower for 7th and 28th October, and devoted to St. Simon, the Apostle, and Pope St. Mark, 336 A.D.

Coleus

Coleus are beautiful foliage plants of immense variety. Among plants with coloured leaves, I know of nothing more easy to cultivate, more effective or more prolific than these, and therefore they are to be strongly recommended. Get a bundle of cuttings at the beginning of the rains, and put them down at once in a partially shaded corner, in soil composed of equal parts of leaf-mould and stable litter, with a sprinkling of sand. But they will grow even in ordinary soil during the rains. I shall take it for granted you are just beginning with your very first batch of coleus cuttings. Well, when those in the ground throw out three or four branches, which they are not long in doing, take of each plant as many cutings as you can, five or six inches long, plant each in an 8-inch pot and see that you sink quite half the cutting beneath the soil. Keep these pots in the shade of your conservatory where they will get plenty of light and rain. As soon as these have in their turn put out three or four branches, you may cut off these too, and increase your supply in the same way, and go on cutting through July and August without scruple. Each cutting will make a beautiful plant for you all through September, October and November. Of course if you don't want hundreds of plants for clumps and borders, you need not cut so much. You will see the new leaves come out in pairs; with your finger and thumb pinch off here and there the newest pair appearing at the *end* of each spray. This makes them throw out more leaves underneath and helps the plant to a *bushy* appearance. If the weather is frosty bring all your coleus under shelter. If you want to have abundant supplies for next season, you must cut up all your pot plants into pieces, and the plant them under some shady trees or close together in wooden boxes or big *nands*. Here they will grow *slowly* but *safely* through the cold and hot weather, and be ready to give you hundreds of cuttings again in the next rains. Don't imagine you will be able to keep any of your old plants r coleus in pots just as they are through the hot weather; these, by the time the rains begin (if they have not died altogether!) will be scraggy and almost leafless; and if you attempt *then* to make cuttings from them, none of them will strike; while those you had cut up in November and December and put into the ground and boxes, &c., will be flourishing plants ready to give you ten-fold more cuttings when the rains begin. (*See* "Hints")

During the rains you will often find a small green worm attack the tender leaves of your coleus plants, and this you must get rid of as soon as possible. Mix a wineglassful of kerosine in a gallon of hot water, and when cool, spray your plants freely with it. This should be done in the evening.

Coreopsis

"Love at first sight," recommends itself, as it is a bright yellow, or yellow and brown annual. Sow in October in boxes, and plant them out when about three inches high. A pretty way of growing them is in small circles round a centre of purple larkspur, with a narrow border of white candy-tuft or white phlox. There are two reasons for growing coreopsis and larkspur together: one is: the colours of the flowers are a good contrast, and character of their foliage is similarly fine and feathery; the other reason is that they will both keep longer in bloom than the other annuals, if you cut away the old flowers before the seed-pods form. (*See* "Larkspur") Wherever these are grown, you will find them appear self-sown the following year. The flowers of these second year self-sown coreopsis will do very well, but thsoe that appear the third year are not worth having, and should be all uprooted directly they appear.

Cornflowers

Their meaning in the Language of Flowers is *delicacy.* You can't do without their elegant blue blossoms, especially as further on you will come across its best companion, the poppy. The *blue* cornflower is what you want, so send for seeds of *Centaurea cyanus,* and sow towards the end of October just where they are to remain, becuase they won't bear transplanting. If you can spare a good big bit of ground, about twenty feet square, sow poppies and cornflowers in lines two feet wide; if not, in small square beds, marking each bed into four smaller squares, and sow cornflowers and poppies in each alternate division. Some of these small squares ought to appear in the space left for annuals in front of your shrubberies. Water along the roots : they won't stand watering from above. But the heavy dews of the cold months keep them going so well, that they don't require frequent watering. Save seed of your cornflowers and let them dry thoroughly in loose muslin bags before putting them away in bottles. Cornflower is set down for May 29th and June 28th, and is devoted to St. Cyril, 275; St. Irenaeus, 202. (*See* "Hints")

Crotons

Crotons are the handsomest foliage plants one can cultivate. I did not say anything about them in the former editions of this book, because you know we beginners intend to grow only such things as are not troublesome! Well, as many have asked me for information about them, let us see what we can do in a small way.

You must remember they like a *moist* climate, so if you live in the North of India, you must have a glass-house, or a well-protected "chick" house for keeping them. In the Southern parts of India they grow in great profusion without the slightest trouble, almost anywhere in the open air.

Cuttings take root quite easily *in the rains,* and should be put down in rich soil in a shady place. When they have rooted, take tham up and plant them in pots or boxes so that you can remove them out of the cold (if you live in Northern India), or you may plant them in your shrubberies and open-air conservatories (if you live towards the South of India), where they will thrive all the year round in the ground.

Crotons should always be watered with a fine-rose watering pot, so that the dust being washed off, the leaves will be able to *breathe freely* and show their lovely colourings.

When planted in pots or boxes, these should be banked up with grass in the winter, for the *roots need protection from the cold.* Public gardens in the Bengal, Madras and Bombay Presidencies will supply you with plants or cuttings, and the Royal Botanic Gardens, Ceylon, sell them at the wonderfully cheap rate of Rs. 2 per dozen plants. Don't forget that all your operations, planting or transplanting, are best performed *in the rains.*

Cyanotis

Cyanotis a well-known ground creeper which you have probably heard called "The Wandering Jew!" It is invaluable in rockeries and covers over ugly bare spaces at once. It does not require any attention, for it has wonderful vitality, and accommodates itself easily, almost too easily, wherever it is stuck in. In any shady place where a quick border is wanted, it looks very nice indeed, if you will pin down the "Jew" with pins of wire, and keep him "wandering" in the right direction. You can't do without it in your conservatory, for its brown striped leaves makes a pretty setting for many things there. It makes a capital groundwork in baskets where you wish to arrange pink, red, or scarlet cut flowers. People who prize it sufficiently to grow it in glass-houses in Europe would be surprised to see how common it is in India. (*See* 'Hints")

Cyperus tenuifolius

Cyperus tenuifolius is a palm-like sedge or easily procurable from marshy places. If it is not to be found anywhere close to your station, by all means buy a pot of it from the nearest public garden; it will cost only a few annas and repay you a thousandfold. It makes a really charming "pot plant" for house decoration, especially if you have no palms. It will keep well all the year round if treated in the following way:– Take three or four pots of 10-inch diameter, put a couple of roots of the palm-sedge in each, place each pot in a kerosine tin, letting the sedge of the pot rest on the edge of the tin, and *keep the tin always full of water.* Having your tins tarred, or painted red or green, keep them round or near the reservoir in your conservatory, where it will come in for some of the evaporation, and keep a row of fern pots in front of the tins to form a pretty bank of green. This palm-sedge must always be kept in the shade, and as it increases very rapidly, the roots should be constantly separated. The fewer roots in a pot, the better will be the condition of the leaves. Always cut away those stems that look dry and yellow, and constantly change the pots used for in-door decoration or else they will droop. Florists in England call it "Palmgrass" or "Umbrella fern!"

Dodonea

Dodonea another "common thing," but how beautiful and how useful! It will form a thick evergreen hedge which is just what you want for that *outer enclosure,* which is to guard the ground you are going to make into a flower garden. At the end of July dig a furrow a foot wide, throwing up the soil on either side to form a little bank, so that rain may not wash away the seed. Sow your seeds in three lines four inches apart, cover them over with an inch of soil, and pat firmly down with the hand. Spread brambles over the furrow to prevent the seeds being trampled upon and leave the brambles there even after the seeds have come up, so that they may be well protected till the dodonea is quite established. Like camphire, or *mehndee,* it ought to have a little water in its first hot weather; after that it will do without watering. It will grow compact, firm and strong with very little clipping and pruning, which is to be done in the same way that you trim your *mehndee.* The new leaves that sprout along the evenly cut top form a velvety, bright green surface, that nothing can surpass in freshness. If you take my advice, this will make the best emerald framing for your garden. If you already have a hedge of it, so much the better: only see that you fill up the *gaps* with fresh sown seed in July. In the hot weather your "common" dodonea will bear abundant bunches of pale green seed-vessels, which you will find a very refreshing-looking decoration for your vases and baskets, or used as garniture for any pink, white, red or yellow flowers. Large bunches of it tied up form a pretty change from the dried grass bouquets we often tire of. For evening wear on black or white dresses, these exquisite celadon clusters are not to be depised. (*See* "Hints")

Dracenas

Dracenas are foliage plants well worth cultivating. They have an immense number of varieties, but as you are only a beginner ask for the *robust* kind first; later on you can get those that will need a little attention. They grow easily from cuttings; give them a *free* soil, that is, a good many crocks at the bottom of their pots, and some sand and powdered charcoal added to ordinary garden soil. When your pots have a number of new shoots coming up all round the old plant, wait till the rains begin, then turn out the contents of your pots, separate the new shoots, planting each in a 10-inch pot, sinking the stem into the soil right up to the lower leaves. These lower leaves that touch the surface of the soil will fall away by-and-bye, but the others will expand and increase into a beautiful torch-like form. The old original plant, which has probably grown into a long, leggy stem, several feet high, cut into pieces about nine inches long and plant in boxes as cuttings for next year. If you wish your *new* shoot planted in the 10-inch pot to grow bigger, transplant it the following year into a bigger pot. Sink some of these pots into your rockeries, and as the hot months will try them they will be all the better if you can dip the top of the plant into water, or hold the pot horizontally over your reservoir and pour a good stream of water over the leaves to give them a bath. This sort of bath is specially good for the pots you keep in verandahs. *Dracenas will not bear frost,* so keep them sheltered in the cold months.

Doruntа

Dorunta is a hardy, large flowering shurb, well worth having. If you haven't any, send for cuttings in the rains, and plant in clumps in your shrubbery or make a small hedge of it. They will grow in any soil where they will get plenty of sun. The hedge will want pruning; but those grown as shrubs need not have more than the extremity of their branches cut away in cold weather, only to form them a little into shape. *Dorunta plumieri* has light mauve flowers in large sprays; as these flowers fall, bright yellow berries form, which when cut and used for in-door decoration, last a long time. *D. plumieri* is very hardy and needs no care after it is established. *Dorunta elisii,* with white flowers, is very pretty indeed and most useful for bridal decorations. (*See* "Hints") This white flowering variety does not grow quite as high as the mauve, and wants a little water in the hot weather. When slightly pruned in winter it keeps in good shrub form. You will, I am sure, be delighted with it, and with the variety of decorations to which it lends itself.

Eglantine *See* "Sweet Briar"

Everlasting

The French "Immortelle" gives no trouble to cultivate, and as it is very useful in dry grass bouquets, plant some of it in one or two small plots in October, just where you intend it to remain. Make holes with your finger, six inches apart, and drop two or three seeds into each. The flowers keep in bloom for months. Those which you intend to use in your dry bouquets should be cut when they have fully expanded. Send to the Himalayan Seed Store, Mussoorie, for a packet of mixed *Helichrysum monstrosum.* Save the seeds of the different colours, and dry in loose muslin bags before putting away in bottles. (*See* "Hints")

Ferns

"The feathery Fern! the feathery Fern!
    An emerald sea it waveth wide,

And seems to flash and gleam and burn
Like the gentle flow of a golden tide;
On bushy slope or in leafy glade,
Amid the twilight depth of shade,
By interlacing branches made,
And trunks with lichens glorified!"

Everybody loves ferns, and everybody is anxious to have around them as many as possible of these refreshing "mysterious" ornaments of the forest glade. In Pliny's time ferns were considered of mysterious origin, for he says of them : "They bear neither flowers nor seed." In later years the idea was that fern-seed was visible only on St. John's Eve (Midsummer, *i.e.*, 24th June).

"But on St. John's mysterious night,
Sacred to many a wizard's spell,
The hour when, first to human sight
Confest, the mystic fern-seed fell."

Ferns are put down to January 29th and February 24th, and are devoted to St. Ethelbert, King of Kent, St. Marcella, 410, and St. Francis of Sales, 1622.

Ferns will grow very well in the plains of India if you know how to take care of them. Year after year you see people coming from the hills with baskets of lovely ferns, because they are under the impression that ferns, like geraniums, should be renewed by fresh stock from the mountains each successive season. A cruel mistake! To send out *jampanies* and coolies in all directions to wrench off and dig up ferns ruthlessly from their natural homes, and bring them to starve and die in the plains, is a barbarism that makes one shudder! As you are a beginner, – and I don't pretend in this little work to give you more than the rudiments of simple flower-gardening,–the most we can hope for with regard to ferns is, that if you follow my instructions, you need not have on your conscience the sin of killing all the ferns you take in hand. August and September are the best months for bringing down ferns from the hills. Some of the kinds you see won't live in the plains, so if you can't recognize those that will bear being transferred, you will surely have some friend who will be able to tell you which are *adiantum, lastrea, cystopteris, polypodium* and *blechnum*. Most of these will thrive down in the plains. Ferns are of two kinds: *Deciduous* and *evergreen* : the former go to rest in the summer; the latter remain green all the year round. I will suppose you have no friend to tell you the classes of the ferns, so you might guide your choice in a small way by remembering one or two points about those you ought and ought not to bring away. The larger kind of ferns with *brown, hairy stem,* as a rule, do not like the plains, so choose those with stems that have silvery white hair and those whose stems have no hair at all. Then there is another class you must avoid, and that is very *fine, lace-like ferns.* These also won't bear living away from their mountain home. When you search for ferns and come across any creeping variety you may safely take them up. Now take notice what is meant by *creeping* ferns : those that let their leaves curve over and take root from the tip, or point, are pretty strong, and some of these are found in the plains, especially two, *Adiantum lunulatum* and *Adiantum caudatum.* In jungles that are shady and swampy you will be sure to find some beautiful varieties of creeping ferns, the best of which is *Goniopteris prolifera,* which will stand all weathers and provide you with the most elegant hanging baskets. The few ferns I have mentioned are to be found *all over India.* Collect your ferns in the afternoon (I mean those you intend to bring down) and leave them in the dew or rain all night in the morning *shake* from the roots as much soil as will come off by shaking and pack them close together in a basket in layers, putting between the layers a light sprinkling of shreds of moss. Shut down the lid of the basket. In this manner, during the rains, your ferns will stand a journey of forty-eight hours. When they have arrived at their journey's end, get ready their pots and trays in this way : the pots should be well washed and the holes below should be opened properly; then small pieces of brick, about the size of hazel-nuts, filled into almost half the depth of the pot; over these put a layer of coir fibre or old moss; then fill up to within an inch of the top with soil composed as follows : – Three parts leaf-mould, one part powdered charcoal, two parts *kunkur* broken up to the size of peas. Let this soil settle by sprinkling well with water. Your pots should be from five to twelve inches wide, according to the size of your ferns. In your trays, which should be lined with tin at the bottom, you won't need more than one layer of brick, since the depth of the trays is not more than five or six inches (*See* "Trays and Stands"); then add the coir and soil as already explained.

Now for the planting of your ferns. Have by you a tin of clean cold water, and as you take each root of fern out of the basket, cut away the bruised leaves and put them on one side, plunge each root into the cold water *for an instant only,* then place it on the top of your soil which is ready in the pots and trays. When you have thus disposed of all the roots turn to the fronds, or leaves, which you have put aside; break up these into small pieces and spread over the roots that are still exposed on the surface of the soil. When you have covered up the roots with their own leaves, then add a layer of about half-an-inch of soil, and in the hollows left between the roots, put bits of *kunkur* and charcoal. It seems rather a troublesome process, but you will be rewarded by soon seeing new fronds peeping out. At first you must water these newly-planted ferns three times a day, and after they have established themselves, twice a day will be sufficient. With "maiden-hair fern" you must have something extra, that is, small *gurrahs* of water should be placed on your trays before you put the soil on, and the fine lacy rhizomes, or roots of the maiden-hair, should be spread over the sides of the *gurrahs,* and kept in their places by the weight of the *kunkur* and charcoal placed here and there.

"Silver fern" you know very well. This again has another kind of treatment. To the soil already mentioned, add a little sand and powdered *old lime.* Silver fern likes a dark place, so put the pots they are in under some overhanging shade. Silver fern grew with me to a height of eighteen inches under this treatment. I kept their pots in grass cylinders three feet high, so they were always cool in their grass-house, and got light *only* from the opening at the top of their house.

In the winter the deciduous ferns will go to rest; remove the pots to the shade of a hedge where they will be thoroughly sheltered from the cold; tear up some moss, and spread a thick lace-work of it over these ferns. The dew in the winter will supply sufficient moisture in the air for them. In the hot weather water *very sparingly* once a fortnight. If these ferns are in health, they will all sprout again on the approach of the rains. Don't throw away any fern as dead until you have tested its vitality for a year. If under all your care it shows no sign of life in that time then you may say *good-bye* to it. Keep your ferns where they will be *quite sheltered from wind* and *sun.* They like air and rain, so an open-air conservatory is the place best suited to them. *Blechnum boreale* is a fern I strongly recommend; buy a root of it from the nearest public garden. It is perfectly hardy and spreads itself in a marvellous manner. Those in fountains in the Crawford Markets in Bombay are an illustration of their name - the "hardy" fern. I have this fern, and maiden-hair, &c., in trays in my conservatory, standing in the same place in all weathers from one year's end to another, growing in the utmost luxuriance. They are at their best in winter. *Blechnum boreale* and *Adiantum caudatum* (creeping fern) are very good for hanging basket, and if planted on the top of the brick pillars I have described (*See* "Stands") they will throw out their sprays, which, if pinned into the cavities all round the sides, will soon entirely cover the pillars.

Your evergreen ferns will languish a little in the hot weather; never mind, give them plenty of water, three times a day if you can, and *leave them alone.* They will all come right when the rains set in. *Transplanting ferns in the hot weather means "sudden death."* The monsoon is the best time for all your fern work. Have, if possible, two sets of ferns - one set to keep undisturbed for show and decoration, the other as a resource to be drawn upon for making new boxes and baskets. All the ferns I have told you about increase and multiply tremendously: so if you have no second set of ferns in reserve, you can easily abstract a root here and there from your "show," withiout any visible gaps. Caterpillars are very troublesome enemies of ferns. Dry ashes sprinkled plentifully are the only protection against them, and fumigation, which you will find described in "Hints." For dying and wiring ferns, also *see* "Hints."

If yiou wish your ferns to look perfectly healthy and bright, you must superintend the planting and transplanting of them yourself, for, as a rule, malis do not understand ferns. A bachelor friend of mine, fond of gardening, went to a good deal of trouble and expense to keep his garden nice and had a captial *mali* to look after his plants. The *mali* really took a great interest in everything committed to his charge, *even ferns.* When the gentleman saw *my* maiden-hair fern, he said : "Good gracious! What do you do to make your ferns grow so well? *My* maiden-hair fern will not grow beyond an inch or two." The next morning this *mali* was sent to me with a basket of his ferns to have the mystery of their backwardness explained. there was a very good basket eighteen inches deep, and there was a *gurrah* of water, and there were signs, and signs only, of maiden-hair fern, fern that the *mali* in his excess of devotion had buried beneath a foot of *pure cow-dung* for soil! If you don't watch your *mali he* also will manure your ferns, and they will at once perish.

A highly cultivated Native gentleman admired everything in my garden exceedingly, except the ferns. When he came to those he said : 'Madam, I can understand your taking trouble with beautiful flowers, and coloured leaves, but *these things* (the ferns) how can you care for them? *They are only common bhagy"* (spinach!). So much for the opinion of an educated Native : then how much can be expected from an ignorant *mali*? Your foolish fondness for ferns will always be beyond his understanding.

Gardenia

By this I mean a common, large shrub bearing most exquisite white flowers with a faint odour, foliage of a brilliant shining green, and known by the long name of *Taberna montana coronaria!* You very probably have some old shrubs of it in your garden; the flowers of these thick, woody old shrubs are not as good as those of new young shrubs. So if you take my advice you will dig up your old bushes *in the rains,* and make new plants by separating the rooted stems or by cuttings. It grows very quickly, and you can get quantities of it in this way.

If you have none of your own, any neighbouring garden, I am sure, will be able to supply you with cuttings. When the flower-buds begin to form at the end of the stems, thin off the leaves. By so doing you improve the size of the flowers. When grown in partial shade the foliage of this gardenia becomes very dense, and the flowers sparse, so see that you give it all the sun and light you can. Each clump or shrubbery ought to have at least two or three of these lovely bushes. If you look at this shrub on a moonlight night, the dazzling whiteness of the blossoms and the bright sheen of the glistening foliage will explain how it has got the native name of *"chandnee," i.e.,* "moonbeam." I don't think these moonbeams are valued as they deserve to be. (*See* "Hints") Prune your shrubs in oval form in the rains, and the branches pruned off should be placed in the shade till rooted; then taken up and planted where wanted. It does not require any particular soil.

Geraniums

Geraniums are very easily propagated by cuttings. In the hills this may be done any time from July to October. In the plains from October to December is the best time.

This charming flower does very well in the plains in the South of India, but in the Northern stations they must be renewed every October. In the hills they do splendidly in open verandahs, and the common kinds don't mind being out in the ground.

Water always at the root, not from the top, and see that there is an extra handful of sand or brick-dust mixed with the soil of each pot.

Gilliflowers. *See* "Pinks"

Grasses

Grasses as a rule are short-live; but there is one grass which is evergreen, and which is sure to delight you – *pogonantherum,* It is a very pretty grass found in the hills, has something of the character of bamboo, but its stems, instead of being stiff and upright, are slender and supple, like thread, and its fine, elegant sprays grow about three feet long, and droop over most gracefully. If you can't get any one to show you which is *Pogonantherum crinitum,* when you are in the hills, perhaps you will be able to find it out from my descriptions, if not you can buy a pot of it for two annas from the Government gardens, Lucknow, as I did six years ago, and so learnt its name. It keeps beautifully green and fresh through the rains and cold weather; in the hot months it dries slightly here and there but not enough to make it look unsightly; in fact it never dies. Plant it in shallow boxes and pans; soil, leaf-mould with a sprinkling of common earth and sand. Keep in entire shade, and well raised from the ground. In a porch facing east I had two boxes of it on rustic stands, and as I watered it three times a day in the hot months and twice a day during the rest of the year, it always looked like a refreshing green waterfall! In my conservatory I have flat pots of it stuck in forks of trees, a place it loves to grow in, in boxes on stands, &c., a veritable "thing of beauty." You will find your pots, &c., very soon fill with roots, so in the rains divide these, putting three small bunches of roots into each new pot. It likes plenty of water from the top; give it light, *but no sun.*

Grass mean *utility,* and St. Timothy, A.D. 304, is the only Saint to whom the Calendar devotes it.

Grevillea Robusta

The Australian "Silk Oak," is a king among foliage shrubs! Let me recommend your procuring at least two of these to plant in the corners of your lawn furthest from your house, or in two shrubberies on either side of your carriage-drive. If you don't already know it, here is Firminger's description of it : –"A most noble object, handsome at all periods of its pyramidal growth, with beautiful dense foliage of fern-like rich, dark-green leaves."

At public gardens you can buy small plants of *Grevillea robusta* from four to six annas each. I bought one for six annas, and planted it in the centre of the front lawn of the Shahjehanpur City Dispensary, and in the third year of its age, it was in splendid condition and twelve feet high!

If your station has frosty nights in the cold weather, your *Grevillea robusta* ought to be protected during its first winter, after that it does not come to any harm. Water well during the hot weather. It is propagated by seed; but I have never tried growing it from seed, as the plants are so cheap.

In warm, moist stations in the South of India it will grow without the least trouble and makes beautiful pot-plants.

Gypsophila

Gypsophila is really a weed found in Northern India, but cultivation has made it a most desirable addition to our annuals, and as an elegant garniture in floral arrangements, you will be charmed with it!

Send to Sutton & Sons, at Reading, England, for seeds of *Gypsophila paniculata,* and sow in October just where you wish it to grow, as it will not bear transplanting. The flowers are white, borne in myriads on fine, grass-like, branched stems, and if you sow a little patch five or six inches across, it will prduce a lovely bush about a yard high, and nine feet in circumference; you must remember this when deciding where you will grow it.

Scatter some of the seed in a bed of mixed poppies, such as *Papaver alpinum* and *Papaver nudicaule,* and the result will be what Whittier calls : –

"An added beauty to the earth."

Heliotrope

Heliotrope or "Cherry pie," can be grown most successfully in the plains under one very simple condition, that is, keeping it raised at least eighteen inches above the level ground. Dion't attempt to grow it from seed. Buy a healthy pot of it in November, and on a sunny site, make a mound quite eighteen inches high, of ordinary earth, to which add a small basketful of leaf-mould and one of powdered bricks. Bank up your mound with *kunkur* or *rori* (burnt pieces of brick from the kiln), – sink your pot of heliotrope just as it is into the middle of the mound; it will rapidly throw out brancehs in all directions. Catch these down by placing pieces of brick on them, taking care to first place a handful of soil on that portion of the branch pressed down under the bit of brick. Branches pinned down in this way in November ought to be well rooted by the end of January. Cut them away from the parent stem and plant where you wish them to grow; but remember that unless you raise their abiding place, in the way I have described, and give them good drainage, they will probably all perish during the following monsoon. Young plants should not be planted out later than the first week in February.

It may help you to know how I managed mine. At the beginning of one November, I bought a potted plant from the public gardens at Aligarh, and planted it in the centre of a high mound. The first season there were layers from this one plant enough to stock a large raised bed; then from this bed the following year layers were taken to form two hedges along my lawn. Nothing of all this heliotrope is lost. Year after year it grows through all the rain, secure in its high place from *water-logging,* which is its one great enemy in the plains. Prune away at the end of the rains all branches that look shabby. These will take root if you plant them in a shady place.

Heliotrope is a native of the Cordilleras of Spain, where it was first discovered by the great French botanist, Jussieu, who was attracted to it by its strong perfume. Struck by the peculiarity of its turning its flowers to the sun, he gaeve it the name of Heliotrope and sent some of its seds to the Royal Garden at Paris, where it was first cultivated in 1740. As the Calendar of Flowers was compiled long before that event, Heliotrope, though it means *devotion,* is not to be found dedicated to any saint. (See "Hints")

Hibiscus

Of this splendid flowering shrub there are many varieties, but I specially recommend three as most effective and beautiful. *H. mutabilis,* flowers very large and very double, changing from white in the morning to brilliant red in the evening; *H. syriacus albus,* flowers very double, of the purest white, more compact petals, but not so large as the preceding; *H. rosa sinensis,* perhaps the most beautiful of all, flowers large, single, bell-shaped, and of a rich Chinese red. These three can be propagated with the greatest ease by cuttings during the rains, and cuttings of *H. S. albus* flower beautifully the following year.

During the coldest months of winter the hibiscus is given to shedding its leaves. At this period prune them to half their height, and put down the cuttings in any place sheltered from frost. They grow in ordinary soil, want very little water when young, and when well established occasional watering only. Rooted plants must be placed where they will have sun, else they won't flower well. Remember to have some of these in your reserve plot as they form a very valuable addition to the list of cut flowers for decorative purposes. Many people regret that the hibiscus shuts up so quickly after being plucked, but in "Hints" you will find a method of keeping them fresh for evening decoration.

All through the rains *H. albus* is an exquisite sight, the stems being loaded with bunches of buds which open in succession. A large red and black beetle is a great enemy to the hibiscus. There is nothing for it but to keep picking them off in the mornings till they entirely disappear.

The native name of hibiscus is *gurhul.* The Calendar marks the 5th December for this flower, and it is dedicated to St. Crispina, 304 A.D.

Hollyhock

This is a very old-fashioned flower, but they are now produced in fine double forms, and in such lovely shades of colour, that you really *must* grow some in parts of your garden where you require tall flowering plants. Sow the seeds in October, and when they have developed three or four leaves, transplant them where you wish them to grow, placing them not less than two feet apart.

In parts of India where the rainfall is not very heavy, Poona, for instance, the hollyhock will grow and flower in the rains as well as in the cold weather.

When the flower-buds form, snip off some from the crowded stems, and cut away the side branches and grow only the centre, single spike. (*See* "Balsams") They want sun, and a liberal soil, so when about to flower, give them a little liquid manure once or twice a week. (*See* "Hints")

Honeysuckle

There are several kinds of these, but the Japanese one (*Lonicera japonica*) is what will best reward you, with deliciously scented sprays of white and yellow blossoms. If you get one good rooted plant place it where it will get plenty of sun, and give it the same soil as that mentioned for roses. Almost every house has *jaffery* screens erected at bath-room doors, if these are strongly supported, the honeysuckle is just the creeper for it, as it loves soap-water. I have a *jaffery* screen extending along the south of the house, covered with a glorious tangle of honeysuckle and Marechal Niel roses. These creepers of scent and beauty get the water from the servants' pantry and wash-up and grow with the greatest vigour in consequence. You must have some of it in your garden. If grown in the centre of a bed a support in the form of an umbrella suits it. I inserted four iron rods, four feet long and three-quarters of an inch thick, round a honey suckle, and put a shelf of bamboo lattice on the top to which the creeper was heloped up with twine. It very soon spread over the flat surface. The top flat surface is what enables it to get a good deal of sun. The more sun it gets the better does it flower.

The scent of honeysuckle is a scent peculiarly its own, and quite unlike any other. It flowers almost all the year round, filling the garden with perfume. (*See* "Hints") Propagate by layers as you do heliotrope. The new shoots sent out near the roots are the best for layering. They will strike any time from July to February. You can't have too much of this delicious creeper, which means *generous and devoted affection. (See* "Scent Sachets")

Inga dulcis or Korkapillee

Though another "common thing," is not to be despised. Sow your seeds during July and August, and follow instruction given for Dodonea.

It will grow into large trees if you will allow it, and grow very quickly too. A small grove of it, with a hedge of dodonea or *mehndee,* is what you will find invaluable for your work-yard, if you have no other shady or retired place to keep your seedlings, and do your potting and transplanting. It gives an equable shade all the year round, slightly more dense than casuarinas, but not dense enough to sut out sunshine altogether. In the cold months the leaves, on its long, regular, narrow branches, have a beautiful purple bloom, like the bloom on grapes, and these branches are useful in many ways for decorations. (*See* "HInts")

Ipomea palmata

The commonest, yet the most useful of evergreen creepers. You see it at every railway station, refreshing the eye in the hottest weather with its bright, fresh foliage, and well deserving its railway nickname of "Porter's joy". Make cuttings nine inches long and plant thickly in any soil where you wish them to remain. The monsoon is the best time to do this, as they will then need no watering. The cuttings will take at any time of year, but must be watered if put down after the rains. Of all creepers, this grows the quickest; excellent for conservatory screens; should be thinned where it becomes too dese, especially when it has reached the top of its support. If grown round posts or pillars, it must be tied in to be kept in compact tidiness. Seeds of the pretty white Ipomea – *Moon creeper* – should be sown in the rains. This can be had, at Lucknow gardens, at four annas per packet. Ipomea means *I attach myself to you.*

Ivy

Ivy *(Hedera helix)* will grow very well in the plains if you know how to treat it. If you are going to bring ivy down from the hills, choose good, stout bits of root; never mind if the leaves don't look fresh and bright, for they must, in any case, all fall when the ivy is transplanted. Wrap up what you select in damp moss, and keep the moss damp during its journey. It will travel quite well among yourferns (*See* "Ferns"), and on arrival, should be plunged into water for an instant and then planted at once *on* leaf-mould in which there is plenty of broken bits of *kunkur.* You will notice I say *on,* not *in* the soil, for the stem should always be on the surface and kept down with small pieces of brick. It will root quickly in the rains, and this is the only time of year you should attempt to bring it down to the plains.

Your rockeries will be the best place for it, and you will find it grow in and out the rock-work and find its way to the tree or trees round which you have built your rockeries. It may then be guided into place with tacks and tiny bits of tape, or left to climb the tree at its own sweet will. The twice a-day watering of the conservatory will be quite enough to keep the ivy damp, and it will reward all your trouble and make a charming variety in your rock-plants, protected here from its chief enemy, the hot wind. A quantity of ivy in my rockeries, planted close by the kerosine tins filled with water -(*See* "Conservatories") – turned some of its young shoots over the edge of the tins and remained immersed in the water all through the hot weather without harm.

Ivy puts out its new leaves in the rains, and these keep beautifully fresh and bright through the winter. In the hot weather it makes no growth, and if you see it looking rather withered, don't think it is dying : leave it as it is. The rains will prove its vitality. If you attempt to transplant it during the hot-weather, it will perish completely. If you come across some particularly well-coloured or clear-veined ivy you wish to make the most of, strike new cuttings according to the method described in paragraph "Delicate Cuttings", but first put some powdered charcoal in the cotton-wool. In the hills, you can do this from March to September. On the plains, during the rains only.

Ivy means *friendship;* the Calendar devotes it to St. Paul, the first hermit, and it is used to mark the 15th of January.

Ixora

Native name *Rookminee,* is an evergreen shrub which is very desiable to have in one' garden. There are several kinds, but three kinds will be sufficient for you to begin with: *Ixora coccinea,* with scarlet flowers; *I. rosea,* flowers coral pink; *I. alba,* flowers white. Send for rooted plants in the rains. They keep in flower all the year round, but are at their best in September and October, and as the blossoms when cut do not fade quickly, they are a great addition to your list of cut flowers. Plant in full sunshine in any common soil, to which a little cow-dung should be added. When the plants are old, thick and woody, the suckers round about should be removed and planted elsewhere. These, put down in fresh soil, will bear flowes much larger than the old parent stock. If you have a great number, put some near your well, or your stables, for, when once rooted, they need no care. In November, cut all straggling branches and prune them into shape. (*See* "Hints")

Jasmine

"My slight and slender Jasmine tree,
That bloomest on my border tower,
Thou art more dearly loved by me,
Than all the wealth of fairy bower.
I ask not while I near thee dwell,
Arabia's spice or Syria's rose;
Thy light festoons more freshly smell,
Thy virgin white more freshly glows".

Lord Morpeth.

India, the home of the jasmine, has many kinds of this sweet flower, but three kinds will be very nice for your modest garden. *J. angustifolium,* the foliage of which is very showy and a beautiful sight when in full bloom in the hot-weather; *J. officinale,* elegant and graceful both in foliage and flowers; *J. syringafolium,* very ornamental in the garden with its constant profusion of star-like blooms. (*See* "Hints")

These grow readily from cuttings, layers, and suckers, which should be planted early in the rains in common soil, enriched with a little manure. When they have once established themselves, they need no attention. *J. officinale* is very desirable over a porch, and if grown as a creeper, should not be pruned; but all the three I have mentioned should be pruned just before the rains, if grown as shrubs.

The jasmine was taken from India to Europe by Spanish navigators in 1560. It means *amiability.*

Kuronda

Kuronda is the native name, and *Carissa carandas* the Latin name of a common shrub. It forms a bushy shrub, like *ixora;* the blossom is of no particular value, but the fruit is lovely!

The berries appear in small bunches in the rains, and look as if they were made of wax exquisitely tinted, from the purest white, through shades of brilliant scarlet, to the richest ruby. The bushes, when loaded with this most uncommon fruit, form a sight, the charm of which is not easily forgotten.

There are two kinds of kurondas – the pink and the green. The former is what you must ask for : the berries of the latter change from green to black, are round, and cannot in any way be compared with the perfect oval of the pink kind.

They are propagated by seed and rootlets, and should be planted in the rains. Water occasionally during their first hot weather, after that they need no attention. Plant in your shrubberies, or in one or two small clumps by themselves; prune after the fruiting season is over.

Lagestroemia Indica

Called by the natives *Gool Fanoos,* is one of the most beautiful of shrubs, and I know none more easy of cultivation. There are three colours - white, pink and mauve, and all can be propagated by cuttings from July to November. They need no special soil and no special watering beyond the first hot season. Plant by carriage drive or shrubberies, pink and white alternately, but keep the mauve in groups by itself. Some of the white and pink should be planted *singly* in the centre of flower beds, and after flowering, these should be pruned down to within eighteen inches of the ground in November, or when they begin to shed their leaves. Tall annuals like poppy, cornflower, &c., may be planted round to hide the bare stumps during the cold season. In the hot weather the lagestroemia puts out its refreshing green leaves, and then from May onwards it is in glorious bloom.

The single ones in beds will throw out their long graceful sprays of bloom, the tips of the lower ones drooping over almost to the ground. Those in the shrubberies need not be pruned lower than four feet. Make use of all your cuttings, of the white especially, for you can't have too much of this in your reserve plot, &c., to supply continuous demands for table decorations, and to prevent the *mali* gathering the blooms from those shrubs you wish to show in all their glory. (*See* "Hints")

Larkspur

Larkspur is a pretty purple annual you must not go without. Sow the seeds in October where you wish them to remain, as they won't bear transplanting. I have already suggested its being grown with coreopsis, but patches of it here and there, in the space forming the border of your lawn, will add to the variety of colour; but remember to plant it rather in the background among your annuals, because it grows tall, sometimes between two and three feet high, and must not overwhelm the low-growing annuals like phlox, pansies, &c. Ask Sutton to send you a packet of the lovely blue larkspur (*Delphinium coelestinum*). These are of a decided, uncommon, *skyblue* and should not be planted near the purple, but by themselves, or in the middle of small beds with borders of low annuals red, white and yellow. Save your seed by plucking and drying the fully ripe pods. Larkspur means *lightness.*

Lilies

> "The Lily's height bespake command–
>
> A fair, imperial flower;
>
> She seemed designed for Flora's hand,
>
> The sceptre of her power".

Under the head of lilies I include *Amaryllis,* as most amateur call them lilies. I strongly recommend these bulbous plants, as they are easy to cultivate, their blossoms are specially beautiful and graceful, and their colouring most varied. As you are a beginner, I shall mention only a few you may take up with confidence and satisfaction. *Polianthes tuberosa,* the most common of lilies in India; *Eucharis Amazonica,* as exquisite pure white lily; *Hedychium coronarium,* a lovely, deliciously-scented lily; and different kinds of *alliums* and *amaryllis.*

Leaf-mould with a little sand is the soil almost all lilies thrive in. Plant your *P. tuberosa* either in pots or in the ground. If you have room, they look well in the border behind your zephyranthes (*See "Zephyranthes"*). They flower in the rains. Cut down each flower-stalk after the flowers are over. If the winter is severe, the leaves also will die down. Those which you grow in pots may be moved into verandahs; stop watering them when they go to rest, and begin again when you see green blades appear above the surface of the soil. At the beginning of the rains you should separate the bulbs which you will find have greatly increased. When the flower spathes begin to form, a little liquid manure at the root will do them good.

Eucharis lilies won't grow in the sun, though they like plenty of light. Plant them in your rockeries, and in pots at the beginning of the rains, and give a little liquid manure when you see they are about to flower, and stand the pots in saucers of water. Let the pots remain standing in water till in winter you see the leaves turning yellow, then remove them to a corner of your work-yard, where they will be protected from the cold, and bury the pots up to their rims in the ground, or bank earth round them. Water *slightly* once a week while they are at rest. As soon as the weather becomes warm, take up your bulbs and plant one in each pot: you will find they have multiplied tremendously. As soon as the new leaves begin to show, water them every day. The leaves ought to grow to a good size and look strong by the time the rains begin, when you must *again transplant them,* and stand the pots in water. Don't use manure till they begin to show signs of flowering, and then only a little, for too much will prevent their flowering.

If you do just as I have advised, you will find that, in two or three years, you will have more eucharis lilies than you know what to do with!

The *Hedychium coronarium* when in flower in the rains is, as a friend of mine called it, *"a perfect poem"*. It may have been the beauty and perfume of this lily that inspired Heine to say :–

"I will steep my fainting spirit
In the Lily's calyx pale,
The Lily in tones that stir it,
A song of my love shall exhale.
That song shall vibrate and shiver,
Like the ever remembered kiss,
That from her lips on mine did quiver,
In hours of divinest bliss".

The tubers of this lily are like rough ginger roots, and spread out vigorously. Don't bury the tubers too deep: one tuber in a 12-inch pot, with an inch of soil lightly sprinkled over, is sufficient. Do this in the hot weather, and keep your pots in the shade. Water them every day, and when the leaves are six or seven inches high, stand the pots in saucers of water. During the rains there will be several stems of flowers sent up in succession from each pot, and each stem will bear a head of buds which will open from three to ten at a time, perfuming the whole of your conservatory deliciously. Cut down each stem after it has done flowering, and when you see no more new stems coming up, take the pots out of the water and place them under a hedge, where they will be protected from cold at night, and yet be able to get warmed by the sun in the day. As the weather warms, the tubers will begin to sprout; turn them out of the pots and separate them. Do this by cutting them with a sharp knife into pieces four inches long. *See that each piece has some root,* and then proceed as above instructed. If you find that your pots are *full* of tubers by August, you may safely separate them again. This lily does not do well in the ground.

Mr. P. Barrie, Mussoorie, N.W.P., is most learned on the subject of lilies and all tuberous plants, and I would advise you to apply to him for all you want in this repect. I am indebted to him for an introduction to many heavenly things in the way of lilies.

The Lily means *majesty. Lilium candidum* is devoted to the Virgin, and marks the 2nd of July, and fourteen other kinds of lilies are devoted to Bishops and Saints in the Calendar. (*See* Carlo Dolci's celebrated picture at Munich.)

Amaryllis are beautiful lilies for both ground and pot culture.

The Government Garden at Lucknow supplies them at Rs. 5 per hundred. Send for a few of each kind at the end of the winter. Those for the ground should be planted in rather a protected part of the garden, where they will get the sun for only a small part of the day; those in pots place in the most open part of your conservatory, and on the edge of your verandahs.

Some will flower in the hot months, some in the rains; all will go to rest at the approach of winter, when you must stop watering. Those in the ground may be taken up and put away in boxes like your caladium bulbs; those in pots may be left under the hedge with your other lilies. Water them as soon as they begin to sprout in the hot weather, and when the flower spathes form, mulch (stir open) the surface of the soil and give a little liquid cow-dung once a week till they have finished flowering. The small bulbs you may plant three in a 10-inch pot; those as large as a good sized onion ought to be placed singly in 12-inch pots.

Alliums are tuberous plants you will be very pleased with; they are easy to cultivate and increase largely from year to year. The white kinds which are valuable for garniture are *Allium Neapolitanum* and *Allium ciliatum.* The coloured ones are: *Allium coeruleum* (blue), *Allium flavum* (yellow), and *Allium descendens* (red). Sutton will send you these, and you must treat them in the same way as your *Amaryllis.* (*See* "Hints")

Marguerite

Marguerite (*Chrysanthemum carinatum*), the French marguerite, the English ox-eyed daisy, is an annual well worth cultivating. Sow the seed in October in boxes, and plant out into beds as soon as the seedlings are three or four inches high. Get a packet of mixed seed, as the white, yellow and variegated look better in the mass than each by itself. They like plenty of sun, and as they grow to a height of two feet, should be placed at the back or in the centre of other low-flowering annuals. Masses grown in diamond-shaped beds, with mignonette borders, look very well. Save the seed from the biggest seed vessels. (*See* "Hints")

Mehndee *See* Camphire

Mignonette

Mignonette (The botanist's *Reseda odorata,* the mali's "minnamint") is just what its name, denotes – "little darling", and much obliged ought we to be to Napoleon for introducing into Europe this delicious little flower from Egypt. Get a packet of "Golden Queen" from England, if you can; if not, from the Himalayan Seed Stores, Mussoorie. In the flower bordering I have advised for your lawn, make room for mignonette, and mix with the soil you have prepared for your annuals a little sand and a handful of powdered *old lime.* You are sure to find somewhere or other in your compound bits of broken plaster which you can utilize for this purpose. Sow your seed in October *where it is to remain.* Have some in your smallest pots for bringing into the house, and keep these pots sunk in the earth, else the flower spikes will not be good. Mignonette likes its roots kept warm.

Seed-pods will form in February and March. Collect as much as you can every two or three days, by spreading a handkerchief near the plants, and knocking off the seeds into it by a rather smart fillip of the finger against the stalks. Mignonette should be watered at the root - not from the top. When cut for vases, you will find mignonette will *grow,* and its flower-buds expand right to the tip of the sprays if you will change the water every day and snip off the ends of the stems. (*See* "Scent Sachets".)

Mina lobata

A very handsome, profusely flowering creeper, intorduced from Mexico; seeds are now obtainable from every public garden. Sow in pots in June, before the rains begin, and water every day, keeping them in the sun. These sown early grow slowly, but the stems become firm and strong. In July, sow another lot. As these creepers do not like to be transplanted, the safest plan is to make holes where you wish the *Mina lobata* to grow, and then crack the pots and sink them bodily into the holes. At the end of July or beginning of August give them plenty of water and full sunlight. The upright flower sprays come in pairs by each leaf, and are shaded from crimson and red, through orange and yellow to white, in a beautiful way. It keeps in bloom right into the hot weather, and seeds profusely. Save seed for the following year. The blossoms of the *Mina lobata* have a virtue possessed by few other creepers; after being gathered, they keep fresh for several days if placed in fresh water every day.

Mina lobata climbs well on lattice-work, on pillars, on dead trees, and spreads over rock-work. (*See* "Hints")

Nasturtium (Tropaeolum)

Always makes a good show, so you must not omit this from your list of annuals. Send for the "Tom Thumb" variety in two colours, scarlet and darkest red (or maroon), and for the climbing variety in yellow. The seeds must be sown at the end of October where they are to remain. Plant the red and scarlet in your borders; two seeds together (in case one does not germinate and so cause a gap) at distances of six and seven inches. Snip off some of the leaves where they are very thick : the blossoms will be the better for it. The yellow climbing sort looks well grown around a small or high mound or trained up the brick pillars described elsewhere. Save the seeds when quite ripe, but dry them before putting away in bottles, because they would otherwise be damp, and not germinate when you sow them the following year. (*See* "Hints")

Nasturtium marks the 7th July, and is devoted to St. Felix, Bishop of Nantes, 584 A.D.

Oleanders

Oleanders (*Rhodion*) have much to recommend them. They are evergreen, are always in flower, want no care after they have taken root and blossom the year after they are planted. In making a new garden, let these be almost your first thing to start with, for they are a great "stant by". They grow in any soil, but a little manure or leaf-mould added to common garden earth improves them. Let me advise your planting them along the outer hedge of your compound, or along your carriage drive, or as a screen for your stables or outhouses. Get cuttings of both white and pink to be planted alternately. These cuttings should be eighteen inches long, and at the beginning of the rains should be planted five or six together, *not singly*, in holes dug at distances of six feet. If you have an eye to in-door decoration, put a clump of the *white* olender somewhere, so that repeated cutting of its flowers won't affect the show in your garden. Just when the rains begin prune your oleanders into shape, and thin out the branches round the bottom. I think the oleanders all pruned to an even height of seven or eight feet look charming! While the rain falls the cuttings will not need watering; but through their first winter and hot weather, you must water them every second day. When your bushes are two years old, they go on bravely and not mind if you never give them any water except once or twice in the hot months. In the Bengal and Bombay Presidencies, in the Central and North-West Provinces they grow luxuriantly with little or no care. In very cold latitudes they do not succed. (*See* Flowers in Southern Stations.) There is no shrub to which I feel so grateful as the oleander for yielding an unceasing suply of flowrs. (*See* "Hints") It can also be pruned so as to grow like a standard rose bush.

Oxalis Wood Sorrel

Oxalis Wood Sorrel, is a bright, showy annual, grown from bulbs. Mr. P. Barrie, Mussorie, will tell you all about them. In the meantime get, in September or October, from your nearest public garden, one dozen bubs of each colour. There are many - red, pink, purple, white and yellow. I may tell you they can be had at Saharunpur public gardens at four annas per dozen bulbs. Use 6-inch pots with good garden soil such as recommended for annuals, put three bulbs in each pot, and keep in shade till the leaves are well formed, then bring the pots into sunlight. They are most useful for filling up empty spaces between big pots along the front of your verandahs, which you naturally wish to have appear as bright as possible. And these pots are also very nice for filling in your rustic trays which you may have on rustic stands near your porch, and elsewhere in bright sunlight.

When they die down after the winter, stop watering, and when the soil is quite dry, turn out the contents of the pots, shake away the soil gently, remove the bulbs, and put them away like your caladium bulbs, taking care to keep the colours separate. If you don't want to use the pots for anything else, you may leave the bulbs as they are, and put way the pots in a safe corner of your verandah till the following September, when you should repeat the above-mentioned process. The canary oxalis (*O. cuprea)* in particular is very attractive, as its lemon colour is different from other yellows of your annuals. Oxalis should be watered at its roots, without the rose to the watering pot.

Oxalis marks the 21st and 22nd of November in the Calendar, and is devoted to the Virgin Mary, and to St. Cecilia, Patroness of Music, 230 A.D.

Palms

I am so glad that now-a-days it is the fashion to bring palms, &c., into our rooms, a fashion set in England by the late Prince Consort.

Send to the gardens at Lucknow and Saharunpur, for a list of palms, if you live in the North of India, where you can get them from 4 annas to Re. 1 each.

If you live in the South of India, you could not do better than send to the Royal Botanic Gardens, Ceylon, for what you want, for there you will get an assortment of twelve different kinds, packed in bamboo pots, for the small price of Rs. 2-8.

Livistona mauritiana, the large fan-shaped palm, is what you generally see used by most people. It is a very satisfactory palm to be undertaken by beginners. Then ther are some others I would recommend as very pretty and effective, and easy to grow, *Calamus Roxburghii, Caryota urens, Kentia Forsteriana, Phoenix acaulis, Thrinax argentea,* etc.

We will suppose you will start with small-sized palms. Put them into 10-inch pots first and give them this soil - two parts leaf-mould, one part common garden earth, and one part composed half and half of pounded *kunkur* and river silt. If there is no river near you, the mud from the bottom of a dried-up pond will do instead of the silt. *Take care there is no manure mixed in with your leaf-mould.* Keep your palms in the shade, and give them plenty of water when first planted. In the rains is the best time to plant them. To keep your palms beautifully fresh and green you must remember two things : give them light but *no sunshine directly on them,* and to keep their leaves free from dust by frequent sponging with clean water. If you have no time to sponge each leaf yourself, the best plan is to douche them in your reservoir. Have a piece of board cut round, of a diameter an inch or two larger than the top of your biggest palm pot; cut a hole in the middle of this board big enough to admit the *trunk* of your palm, cut this board right across into two pieces, then fit it on to the top of your palm pot and tie it down securely. Your *mali* can then turn the pot topsy-turvy, and douche the palm in your reservoir quite safely. This is the easiest and most effectual way of clearing off the dust from the pores of your palm leaves, and, as I said before, to free them from dust is to keep them healthy. This should be done once a week in the hot weather; in the winter once in two or three weeks, *but alway in the morning in winter.*

Never keep your palms shut up in your drawing-room *at night;* they can't live without air; so, before shutting up the house, have your palms put right out into the open air in the hot weather and rains; and under a tree in the shelter of the conservatory, or in your verandah, in winter. Palms kept in-doors constantly will have a tendency to look *flat,* with their leaves curving downwards. If this happens to yours, you must remove them to hospital, *i.e.,* your open-air conservatory. They are pining for *overhead light,* which the ceiling of your rooms shuts out from them completely, therfore you must keep them in hospital till the light from above in your conservatory draws up and restores the leaves to a more upright and natural postion. Always cut away sharply with a knife any broken, old or disfigured leaf.

The palms you first plant in 10-inch pots should the following year be put into 12-inch pots, and the next year promote them to 14-inch pots. *Always transplant in the rains.* The sizes I have given are the best-sized pots for rustic stands and for easy moving in and out of rooms. In the 14-inch pot they will grow to a good size and have ten or twelve well developed leaves from twenty-four to thirty inches long. In tubs and in the ground they will grow much larger. Palms are always valuable, and therefore should always be taken care of.

Pansies

From the French *Pensee (Viola tricolour).*

"And there are pansies, that's for thoughts". – Shakespeare.

Sow the seed in your boxes in October (*See* "Seed Sowing") in ridges well apart, for, since they do not all germinate at once, you should have plenty of room to take up those which have five or six leaves, without injuring others which are still undeveloped. The soil for pansies ought to be rich and light, so to the soil already advised for annuals, add just a little more old cow-dung and sand. Take up your pansies as soon as they show four or five leaves, and plant four in each seed-box, and keep them in the shade till they are double the size; then plant out in your beds and keep a good many to plant singly in 6-inch pots, for placing which you will have many opportunities. For porch-steps, verandahs, &c., your little pots with single pansies will make a delightful show of colour. These pots should be put in the open air at night, and frequently changed. If you wish to keep your pansies in flower for a long time, you should snip off the withered blossoms before the seed-pods form. They belong to the violet family, and throw out suckers at the roots, so if among your plants you find some particular kind you would like to have more of, take up the plant and divide it at the root, planting them at once.

When you see the leaves of your pansy plants turning yellow, it is because they have too much manure, or the drainage is clogged. Take up your plant and remedy the defect. Those pots from which you wish to save seed should be set aside when the flowers begin to wither, each colour by itself, and tiny squares of *fine* muslin tied over the seed-bearing stems.

The pansy marks the 13th of March, and is devoted to St. Euphrasia, 410 A.D. (*See* "Hints")

Petunia

Petunia is one of the most necessary of pretty and easily cultivated annuals. Get one packet of white and one of mixed colours, and sow in boxes after the 10th of October, and when grown to two or three inches high, plant them out in your beds and borders. Petunias grow to a height of about eighteen inches, and look effective if set against the raised bank, on the top of which I have advised you to keep your heliotrope and chrysanthemums. The white ones seem to keep longer in flower than the coloured, and you will find if you grow them in alternate lines with your sweet-peas, or to border centres of sweet-peas, the combined perfume will be delicious, and the effect of colour very pleasing.

If you plant your petunias in beds and borders where you wish them to grow closely and compactly, pin down the long sprays with bits of wire bent like big hair-pins. If grown as single plants, pinch off the ends of the branches till the plant attains a bushy appearance.

Petunias are very hardy, and flower all through the cold and hot weather. They die down in the rains, but come up of themselves the following winter. The flowers of the self-sown seed plants do very well the first year, but after that they are poor, so it is better to get fresh seed. (*See* "Hints")

Phlox Drummondi

"The indispensable ornament of an Indian garden", is what Firminger rightly calls this dear little annual. It grows low, so must be put in front of annuals that grow higher. Get some packets of mixed seed, and if you want a veriety for table decoration, send for a packet of dark-red and one of pink. Sow in October in separate boxes. When the plants are two or three inches high, take them up and plant the mixed colours in beds and borders, and the red and pink in patches by themselves (for cuttings) and in flat boxes of your rustic stands; also in small pots for your verandahs and porch,– a good many, so as to admit of their being changed from time to time. Phlox, like petunia, will sow itself, but you must save seed the first year, because the flowers of those that come up self-sown are not so good.

Among your mixed kinds you may see some you particularly like; you can make cuttings from these, or take up the entire plant carefully and divide the roots.

Ask Sutton to send you seeds of the perennial phlox, and plant these in small clumps in corners of your shrubberies, where they will be sheltered from the hot wind. These will grow as tall as your larkspurs, and will keep in bloom longer than the dward philox.

In one of my gardens I had an oblong plot at the back of the house, which I grassed over and planted with a small rosary, each rose-bush at a distance of six feet from the other. This grass-plot rosary had a 9-inch border of red alternanthera, against the inner side of which was a 9-inch border of mixed phlox. This plot, from January to May, was a sight pleasant indeed to the eye. It was watered by the hand, and the grass-cutters kept the grass clipped low. (*See* "Hints")

Pilea muscosa

Pilea muscosa is a pretty weed often mistaken for a fern. You will get plants of this at the gardens at Saharunpur at six annas each. If you start with two plants in your damp, shady rockeries, you wil have quantities the following year. It creeps and roots itself very satisfactorily, and you will find new plants growing on the stones where it had shed its seeds. It is one of the prettiest evergreens you can have in your rockeriest; it is easily propagated by layers, and most useful in table decoration. (*See* "Hints".)

Pinks

Pinks (*Dianthus sinensis*) are the old-fashioned "gilliflowers" of Chaucer, Spenser and other old poets. Shakespeare makes Perdita say-

> "The fairest flowers of the season are our carnations and streaked gilliflowers."

Pinks having flowers and foliage differing completely from other annuals, form a pretty variety. Sow in boxes in October and plant them out when they are about three inches high into beds and borders. Single plants at equal distances in among your mignonette look very pretty. Keep a good many to plant singly, or three in a pot for porch and verandah decoration. The pinks in pots, if kept where they can be sheltered from severe sun and heat, will flower on into the rains; the other flowers of this family - carnations, &c., you must not attempt till you are a more experienced gardener. Pinks will keep in flower a long time, especially if you cut away the old flowers before the seed-pods form. Set aside some for saving seed.

The pink mean *pure love.* It marks the 4th of June and is devoted to St. Quirinus, Bishop, 304 A.D.

Plumbago

Plumbago is a pale blue flower growing in extremely elegant bunches, and well worth cultivating. It grows quite easily from cuttings and division of roots in any part of India where the winter is not severe. Have several small beds with half-a-dozen shrubs of this lovely blue flower, and sow seeds of the scarlet poppy between. Keep the shrubs only about two feet high by pruning in June and October. (*See* "Hints")

Poppies

"The ancients who regarded *Sleep* as the healer of all woes, the great comforter of the world, gave him for his only ornament *a wreath of poppies*".

When sending for seeds, ask for *Papaver orientale.* This is the bright scarlet poppy with dark centre, which one always associates with cornflowers and wheat (*See* C. and W.). Get also a packet of mixed *eschscholtzia,* the Californian poppy, of all sorts of brilliant colours. As you cannot transplant poppies, sow the seeds where they are to remain. In the "Cornflower" paragraph, you will see how I advise sowing them in alternate lines and in beds, and see also paragraph "Gypsophila," whose fine white blossoms show up the colours of the poppies most beautifully. Have a spare patch in your reserve garden for cutting. Fortunately, the poppy does not deteriorate, so save your seed every year. The seeds of poppies are very small, and the Indians use them as the smallest measure of weight, just as the English use barleycorns and call them "grains". (*See* "Hints")

It means *consolation,* marks the 15th, 17th and 24th of May, the 18th and 20th of June, and is devoted fo five saints in the Calendar, among whom is St. Paschal, 1592 A.D.

Portulacca

Portulacca one of the most varied and brilliant of low-growing annuals. Sow in October where it is to remain. You must find room for small patches of it between the roses in your rosaries, and at intervals in grass borders, &c. The reason why I don't recommend their having conspicuous beds to themselves, is that their brilliant blossoms are at their best only while the sun is shining on them. When the sun goes round to the west, the portulacas close in the shade, so that their beauty is not visible to those who come into the garden only in the cool of the evening. But in winter there are many days when one can bear the mid-day sun with comfort, and you will then find what a "thing of beauty" the portulacca is, though it may not be a "joy for ever". In tubs and large *nands* where I had foliage plants, &c., growing in the sun, I scattered some portulacca seed. They flowered beautifully, and formed such a pretty *setting* to the centre plant. Save the seed by gathering before the pods are *quite dry,* else they will burst and be lost. Dry the tiny pods in muslin bags before you put them away in bottles.

Quisqualis Indica

Commonly known as the Rangoon creeper, is a really beautiful evergreen. You may already possess it, if not, some of your neighbours will gladly spare you a root or two. *It needs no care,* a grand virtue in a plant that will afford you flowers all the year round; it can be grown in many ways. I had a big one in a corner of my lawn, among foliage shrubs, which was kept round, compact, and shrubby by always having the old wood pruned away. Then I allowed quisqualis to climb up some camphire (*mehndee*) along my reserve plot, and it formed a thick, shady, permanent *overhanging* hedge, behind which my reserved violet plants, on a bank, grew safely in the rains, and in the shade of which I kept newly potted plants. On the sunny side of your conservatory plant quisqualis here and there to supplement your ipomea, because the broad leaves make a strong shield against the cold blasts of winter and the hot winds of summer. Nail up quisqualis with large nails and wire stretched from one nail to the other against outhouse walls, or along boundary walls, and you will be more than recompensed by the result. Quisqualis throws out suckers in all directions : take these up in the rains, and plant in gaps in hedges; it is most valuable in table and in-door decoration. (*See* "Hints")

Roses

Roses grow wonderfully well in the Central Provinces and the North-West Provinces, and, after all, do not need very much care. But even if the rose were a difficult flower to cultivate, its rare and perfect beauty would be worth the greatest trouble, and no garden can be complete without the "Queen of flowers." Anacreon, the poet of love, says :–

"Resplendent Rose! the flower of flowers,
Whose breath perfumes Olympus' bowers;
Whose virgin blush of chastened dye,
Enchants so much our mortal eye."

There are five or six hundred kinds of roses to be seen in the different public gardens, so it is not an easy matter to choose which you will have, especially as there are some roses known to different persons by different names. However, as you are a beginner, twenty-four different roses will be enough for you to start with, if you have only the small garden mentioned before; but if you have the larger one I have also described, you might send for three or four of *each* of the kinds I recommend.

Pink Roses

1. *La France*
2. *Captain Christy*
3. *Beauty of Waltham*
4. *Sauvenir d'un Ami*
5. *Souvenir de Malmaison Rouge*
6. *Victor Verdier*
7. *Edward's Rose*

Red Roses

1. *Monte Christo*
2. *Black Prine*
3. *Alfred Colomb*
4. *Firebrand*
5. *General Jacqueminot*
6. *Horace Vernet*

White Roses

1. *Acidale*
2. *Amabilis*
3. *Citrodora*
4. *Coquette des Blanches*
5. *Devoniensis*
6. *Madame Noman*

Yellow Roses

1. *Augusta Vacher*
2. *Elise Sauvage*
3. *Gloire de Dijon*
4. *Marechal Niel*
5. *Marie Van Houtte*
6. *Solfaterre*

Of all which I have mentioned you can obtain well-rooted plants at eight annas each from the Lucknow and Saharunpur gardens. Cuttings are two annas each; but if you are at any distance from the gardens, I won't advise getting cuttings, as you can't depend on their travelling safely. But if you are only an hour or two by railway journey distant from the gardens, you may venture on cuttings. (*See* "Rose Cuttings")

But whether you send for rooted plants or cuttings, do not begin earlier than 10th October or later than the end of November – the earlier date for the Central Provinces; the later date for the North-Wester Provinces. I say this, as I find the heat begins sooner in the Central Provinces than in the North-Western Provinces : so you must give your new plants as much of the cold weather as possible to establish themselves before the summer begins. So that you should know exactly what you are sending for, I had better give you a short.

Description of Roses which I have mentioned

Pink Roses

La France, beautiful in all respects and a constant delight. She is in fact queen of all pink roses. Deliciously scented, of good shape, large, and very generous. Though she sends out her best blooms in the winter, she gives you some flowers in the rains too. Her monsoon roses are better in the Central Provinces than they are in the North-Western Provinces.

Captain Christy comes next – a fitting pair to *La France,* of exactly the same shade of pink, but differently shaped petals, large and free. He frames his magnificence in rich bronze leaves which cluster close up to his petals, and like a soldier, *Captain Christy* holds himself erect and firm. He is finer full-blown than in bud.

Beauty of Waltham is a fine rose, of rich, satiny pink, slightly deeper in tint than the two foregoing roses. Its glossy petals curve outwards, and it bears flowers plentifully. Does not grow quite as high as *La France* and *Captain Christy.*

Souvenir d'un Ami grows to the same height as *Beauty of Waltham,* has glossy green leaves, of bushy habit, flowers plentifully, an elegant fresh pink rose, lovely in half-blown bud.

Souvenir de Malmaison Rouge, an old-fashioned climbing rose, whose charm is ever new. A very vigorous rose, needs some support, profuse flowerer, cuttings root very easily.

Victor Verdier, a clear, bright, pink rose, quite different in tint and shape from the five other pink roses mentioned. Erect in habit and very showy.

Edward's Rose. – It goes without saying that you will have plenty of the hardy, common pink *Edward's Rose,* or *monthly rose,* to perfume the garden, though ladies usually do not care to use it for decorations in the house on account of its pronounced and some what crude colour.

Red Roses

Monte Christo is a large dark-red rose, close-petalled, and exquisite perfume, hardy growth, and with handsome foliage.

Black Prince, as its name denotes, is the darkest of red roses. Give it all the sun you can, and an old nail or two buried near its root. Iron is supposed to enhance its colour. When cutting the blooms of this rose, do so in the morning when the bud is half-open, and it will retain a pretty shape to the end. When full-blown on its own bush, its petals curve downwards and then it is not so dark as when half-blown.

Alfred Colomb is a well-shaped, bright red rose, beautiful in all its stages - from the small bud to the full-blown flower.

Firebrand is a dark-shaded red rose of good shape, and gets its name from being conspicuously attractive. A strong, erect-growing rose.

General Jacqueminot is one of the good, old-fashioned, never-failing rose, with regular petals. The General is gallant enough to give you some blooms even during the rains!

Horace Vernet is a model rose, over which any artist might become inspired! To me it is the best of all red roses. Its perfume is delightful, and nothing can eclipse its beauty when in half-blown bud. See that it gets liquid manure weekly when its buds begin to form, and save every cutting carefully.

White Roses

Acidale is a *tea-rose,* which I have classed among the white ones, as its faint, flesh-pink tint is too pale to class it among the pink roses. It is one of the sweetest of *tea-roses,* flowering profusely all through the rains and winter, and lends itself to all sorts of arrangement in bouquets, &c. Its profuse sprays of buds and new leaves form a pretty decoration in themselves.

Amabilis is another *tea-rose,* Similar to the preceding in habit, but thicker petalled, and, perhaps, of a slightly deeper flesh tint. I might coin a word in favour of this rose, and call it a *resource-full* rose! Its buds are borne plentifully on longish stems, and may be freely cut to arrange as garniture with other roses whose buds are too precious or too few to be gathered at an early stage.

Citrodora, a pure white climbing rose, you will be delighted with. It is strong, grows quickly, and bears a profuse quantity of flowers in never-ending bunches. Give it support, and prune it sparingly in October.

Coquette des Blanches is a very satisfactory miky-white rose, full and cupped in form, given to hang its head rather coquettishly, very hardy and useful; it seems to be continually in bloom.

Devoniensis, a sweet old-fashioned rose, whose hal-opened buds are considered to be so perfect in tint and form as to make it a favourite model to French artificial flower-makers. Flowers profusely, has very pretty bronzy-green foliage, and grows easily from cuttings.

Madame Noman, a perfectly white rose, another model of the artificial flower-makers. It is beautifully shaped, of dwarf habit, has pale green leaves, flowers liberally, and possesses to a great degree the strong perfume of the real Persian "otto of rose".

Yellow Roses

Augusta Vacher is a handsome rose, of rich coppery yellow, full and firm, and beautiful from bud to full-blown flower. Get this rose from the Saharunpur gardens.

Elise Sauvage is sure to please you. She bears flowers in abundance, tender-petalled, full and cupped, of a pale creamy yellow, darker towards the centre. A rose that looks particularly well in vases mixed with heliotrope only.

Gloire de Dijon. – This pale, apricot-tinted rose is a climber of great strength. It grows very easily on support, and loves *soap-water!* You will find its blooms improve very much if you could manage to grow it where it will get the soap-water running from the bath-room spout. Bears a profusion of flowers. A most satisfactory rose.

Marechal Niel, a grand rose, *large* and intensely yellow, strong and quick growing. You must have quantities of this rose, for it is so reliable. I planted three cuttings of Marechal Niel together on a side of the house where it got the soap-water from a bath-room channel. I gave it strong support, and in its third year, in the month of February, I counted more than four hundred blooms at one time on this bush! Cut away old wood in October.

Marie Van Houtte. – Whatever rose you may do without, do not omit this lovely lady from your list. In her you will find a variety of tints possessed by no other rose : her petals of glossy white, canary, and yellow, melt into apricot pink in the most fascinating way. The buds are at first canary, and as they expand, the petals multiply tints of yellow and pink, till, when full-blown, the colour defies description. It blooms plentifully, and cuttings take easily.

Solfaterre is another yellow climber, not so luxuriant as Marechal Niel, of a paler yellow, a more expanded flower of very pleasing form, and a very free flowerer. It is a desirable rose, for it grows anywhere and needs very little care. A great many buds form on each spray, quite a bouquet in itself. Should be pruned slightly in October.

I must ask you to cultivate one more rose, viz., *Sweet-briar,* the *Englantine* of the poets. It is the emblem of "poetry", and in the Floral games, a wreath of it was bestowed on the prize-winner in compositions on the charms of study and eloquerce. Its blossoms have no particular virtue, but the leaves of a bush will send its perfume a long way; sprays of it in a vase will perfume a whole room. It is excellent for pot-pourri. Cuttings of it will not grow, but you can easily propagate it by layers.

Budding of Roses, I won't say anything about here; it is a process you can only attempt after some experience, and then you can refer to more advanced books already recommended. (*See* "Treatment of Roses")

Russellia

There are two kinds, *Juncea* and *Floribunda,* both pretty and effective. *R. Juncea* is to be found in almost every garden, so if you haven't got it, your neighbours may be able to spare you a root or two. I have seen it growing in huge tangled masses in neglected gardens, where it never got a drop of water except what was rained upon it in the monsoon. At the beginning of a garden walk make, in July, a hollow brick pillar (described elsewhere) on each side of the path, fill it with soil composed half and half of common earth and leaf-mould, pour water on the soil to make it settle, then place your *R. Juncea* on the top, letting its long stems trail over the sides of the pillar. It will root itself wherever the stems come in contact with the ground. Take up these rootlets, and if you have a *pucca* water-course near your well, plant them along it. Give those in the pillars occasional watering in the winter, and as much as you can spare in the hot months. *R. floribunda* may be treated exactly in the same way. It is very pretty for in-door decoration, and keeps in bloom for a long time. Prune slightly after the rains. (*See* "Hints")

Saxifrage

You can bring this down from the hills, or you can buy a pot of it (*Saxifraga sarmentosa*) for four annas from any public garden. In rockeries it is invaluable, forming such a pretty velvety covering for border stones One rooted plant will in one season incrase ten-fold; *kunkur* is what it loves to grow upon in the plains, so if it is once established where the rock-work is kept cool, you will find it come out in great force in the rains and continue its silvery green through the winter. It does not like the hot weather, and at that time shrinks back into sheltering crevices. Grow some in flat pots in hanging baskets; but when the hot winds begin to blow, take down these pots and sink them in hollows in your well shaded rockeries. When planting new roots among the *kunkur* or burnt brick, give it a slight sprinkling of leaf-mould. It propagates itself by suckers, which it throws out in all directions.

Saxifrage marks the 12th of April, and is devoted to St. Zeno, Bishop, 380 A.D.

Selaginella

Is a beautiful, tender, foliage plant, between a moss and a fern. You will find many kinds in the hills, if not, they can be bought for a few annas from any public garden. Send for the following kinds: *S. denticulata, S. helvetica, S. rupestris,* and *S. mutabilis.*

Use soil similar to that recommended for ferns, and plant in small pots. Sink these pots in the crevices of your ferneries; the leaves will spread over the rock-work in the rains, but in the winter you will have to take up the pots and keep them warm in your verandahs.

Snapdragon

Common, old-fashioned flower as it is, you must not despise, for it lasts fresh and bright for such a long time, both in your borders and in your vases. Ask Sutton & Sons for their splendid *Antirrhinum grandiflorum.* The low-growing "Yellow Prince", too, will give you a lovely glow of colour in the garden, and plenty of bloom for in-door decoration. Sow seeds in October, and transplant into borders, beds and pots when two inches high. They are very hardy, and if some last right through the year, transplant into fresh soil after the rains.

Sweet-pea

Is what you ought to have in abundance! Send for one packet of pink and one of mixed *Lathyrus odoratus* (Latin for sweet-pea).

Since the publication of the Second Edition of this book, I find there are so many *new* shades of sweet-pea not yet known in India, that I must advise your writing to Sutton for some of them.

The pink is the nicest for in-door decoration, purple being a colour that does not show well at night. Both pink and purple are equally sweet, and should be sown in October, wher there is plenty of sun, in a rather open spot, where it can fill the air with perfume. Put the pink sweet-pea by itself in furrows a foot wide. with *correopsis* in the spaces between the furrows; the peculiar pink and yellow of these two flowers have a very pretty *apricot* effect of colour. The seeds should be sown one by one, making a hole two inches deep, for each seed, at distances of five or six inches. When the peas are about seven or eight inches high, stick in brambles, twigs or bamboo sticks, three feet high; if you put the latter, you should have a line or two of twine interlacing the sticks to give the peas a ladder.

Two packets of seed the first year will be sufficient to give you six times the quantity of seed for the following year. They sow themselves very satisfactorily, but you should save some of the seed for other spots.

Seed-pods form very quickly, and if you wish your pea-blossoms to last as long as possible, you must snip off a great many of the pods as soon as you see them begin to form. See that your twigs or bamboos are all of the same height, to avoid an untidy up-and-down look.

Sweet-pea marks the 17th of July, and is dedicated to St. Marcellina, 39 A.D. (*See* "Hints")

Tecoma Grandiflora

Is a fine creeper that will please you very much. It has extremely pretty foliage, and its bunches of handsome, tawny-orange bells are very uncommon. Sow the seeds in March in a sunny place, in the centre of a bed that is now bare of its winter annuals. Make a support for it similar to that advised for honeysuckle. It will shed its leaves in the cold weather, so then remove the supports, cut in the stems to within eighteen inches of the ground, and let tall annuals hide the leafless tecoma which will be in its glory when the annuals fade. It will send out suckers during the rains : these should be taken up and planted elsewhere. Save the seed.

Tecoma stans

Is a very pretty shrubby tree, which you may probably have somewhere in your compound. If not, plant seeds of it in your shrubberies in the month of March. It has very pretty foliage, and its bunches of yellow flowers afford you very effective decoration through the hot weather. Save seeds when they begin to dry, and plant in your outer hedge near the road, or at the back of your outhouses, in March.

Thunbergia

Handsome, evergreen creepers, you will find very useful. There are two you may send for : *T. grandiflora,* flowers blue, grown from layers in the rains, develops into the densest of creepers. Should be grown at a distance from the house, as it covers the tallest trees and gives the effect of ivy-covered ruins. *T. laurifolia,* pale mauve flowers, in bloom almost all the year round : not so dense as the former. Should be pruned in the winter. Sow seeds in the rains.

Tradescantiae discolour or bicolour

Is an ornamental foliage plant, something like a cactus. You will know it by its long-pointed leaves, being green on the upper and purple on the lower surface. It is very common, but I mention it for several reasons : it grows just where you please. Two or three in your rockery make a pretty variety, and it is very useful for in-door decoration.

You *may* find it somewhere in your garden, if not, some neighbour will probably have more than he knows what to do with, and may spare you a root or two. Plant one or two on the top of brick pillars which mark the entrance to pathways, and let some creeper like *thunbergia* be trained round it. Have a good big clump of it somewhere in your reserve plot for decorative pupose. Always cut away side shoots, and pick out withered leaves, &c., that may lodge between the broad leaves of the *tradescantia.* Keep it bright and fresh by watering with the rose of the watering-pot. Propagate by cuttings. (*See* "Hints")

Tropaeolum *See* **Nasturtium**

Verbenas

If you once saw verbenas growing in full vigour, you would understand why I *strongly* recommend them. Ask for seeds of pink, deep red, and white. I don't advise purple and mauve, because these two are inclined to overwhelm the others. Sow seed in boxes any time in October and November. Those sown later, flower longer into the hot weather. Take up the plants when two or three inches high, and plant in some *raised* beds with broken bricks between the roots. Verbenas don't like quite level ground. They are very pretty in raised borders banked with grass, and a pretty effect is also made by having beds in *three tiers* : red verbena on the lowest, pink on the next, and white on the third, pinning down the trails to preserve the even lines of colour.

Verbenas grow thickly and quickly and seed themselves; save seed in the hot weather. They will look scraggy and withered in the rains : cut away the dead branches and put in cutting of *amaranthus m. ruber,* or coleus. These will make your beds look gay during the rains, and just as these are cut and transplanted (*See* "Coleus"); in the cold months you will find your new verbenas coming up plentifully. Take them up and freshen the soil (soil for annuals) and re-plant. Have some in your reserve plot for in-door use. (*See* "Hints")

Violets

Are emblems of *modesty* –

"It has a scent as though Love for its dower
Had on it all his odorous arrows tossed;
For, though the Rose has more perfuming power,
The Violet (haply 'cause' tis almost lost,
And takes us so much trouble to discover)
Stands first with most, but always with a lover."

– Barry Cornwall.

Get roots of this dear little plant in October. I would not advise your raising it from seed. A few dozens to begin with will cost very little, and the following year you will find they have more than trebled in number. To your soil for annuals, add a little sand, for violets hate heavy, cloggy soil. For pots, the flat, saucer-like pots (*pir-ritch*) are the best. Put a layer of broken bricks at the bottom, fill up with soil to within an inch of the brim, water to make the soil settle, then plant three in a pot, and sprinkle the surface with half-an-inch of soil. These pots ought, if possible, to be dept on the *north* side of the house where they will get the night dews, plenty of light and only a little, say an hour, of actual sunshine. The blossoms of plants, kept in this position, will be plentiful and of a good large size. *I don't manure my violets,* for in my humble opinion, it promotes too much leaf and expedites decay in the rains. In the monsoon, bring your violet pots into the verandah, give them air, light and all the sun-warmth to be had. You will lose a good many; never mind, don't touch them now, but, at the beginning of October, turn out your violet pots.

You will find that many of them which are decayed on the surface have still some vitality left below. Shake your roots quite free from the old soil, and separate the many rootlets you will discover to have formed round each original plant. There will be a great deal of old, lengthy roots, clip these off with scissors to within three inches of the plant, fill up your pots with fresh soil, and plant three in a pot as before.

You will have three times as many violets as you started with. Prepare a *sloping bank* on the north side of your conservatory, round a shady tree, or under the hedge of your work-yard. Do not forget to have the lower half of the bank composed of broken brick to admit of free drainage, especially during the rains. Use the same soil as for the pots, and plant at distances of five inches. Year by year your plants will increase; find new places for them, for you can never have too many of their delicious blossoms. Water every evening in the winter and hot weather, and only occasionally at a break in the rains.

The violet marks the 17th and 20th of March and the 10th of April, and is dedicated to St. Gertrude, Abbess, 626, St. Wolfram, Archbishop of Sens, 720, and to St. Mechtildes, Abbess, 1400 A.D. (*See* "Hints")

Wheat

Will be required to mix with your poppies and cornflowers. Give your *mali* a couple of annas, and tell him to cultivate a small patch for you near his own private vegetable garden. He will know when and how to sow this better than you can instruct him. The green ears of wheat are best with your poppies and cornflowers, but the fully ripe yellow ears you must save for your bouquets of dried grass, in which they will be pretty variety. (*See* "Hints".)

Yucca gloriosa

Is a strikingly beautiful object when in full bloom in the rains. If you have none, and your neighbours cannot spare you two or three shoots, you can buy plants of it in the public gardens at four annas each. Plant in the rains, with moderately rich soil, and where it will get the full blaze of the sun. If your lawn is big enough to admit of clumps of foliage plants at its corners, certainly have *Y. gloriosa* among them, if not, plant them in your shrubberies. If you have a very old bush of it, unearth the whole, separate the off-shoots, and plant singly where required, sinking the stem into the soil so that the lower leaves lie flat upon it. At the end of the hot weather cut away two or three rows of the lower leaves, and bank up the bare stem with fresh soil. The severed leaves may be dried and the fibres used for tying-up purposes. Every year the plants should be treated in this way, and the stem cut down after the flowers have ceased. I recommend *Y. gloriosa* not only because it is a magnificent ornament to the garden, but because its lovely blossoms are particularly useful for decorative purposes. (*See* "Hints")

Zephyranthes

Are small, pretty, pink and white lily-like plants flowering in the hot weather and rains. They can be had at public gardens at six annas per pot. Get Z. *candida* (white flowers) and Z. *carinata* (pink flowers). Plant the white along your grass border, your pink in 6-inch pots, three bulbs in each. Do this in April, and water when planted and when you see the bulbs begin to sprout. (Earlier in the Central Provinces and later in the North-Western Provinces.) These pretty things some call "Star of Bethlehem" and "Indian Crocus". The flowers will come out in May, June and July, and then they will go to rest. Take up the bulbs, which you will find have much increased and put them away like your caladium bulbs, to plant the following year. Water should be withheld when the leaves begin to wither. (*See* "Hints")

Zinnias

Are really showy and satisfactory flowers to be grown during the rains in some of the beds that will then be bare of the winter annuals. Send to Sutton & Sons, Reading, England, for their mixed double *zinnia* seeds, with which you will be charmed. Sow some of the seeds in boxes in the shade at the beginning of the rains, and some a little later, about July, because if your weather is not intensely cold after the rains, you will find some of your later zinnias will continue blooming into the winter. When your seedlings are two or three inches high, plant them out in masses, at distances of nine inches, where they will get plenty of sun. Zinnias have some lovely shades of colour scarcely seen in any other flowers except dahlias. They make the garden gay during the rains, and are very useful as cut flowers. (*See* "Hints") Save the seed, dry in muslin bags before putting away in bottles.

The zinnia marks the 14th of August, and is dedicated to St. Eusebius, third century, A.D.

HINTS

Useful and Ornamental

Pots for Verandahs

Can be placed to great advantage if a low wall is made along the edge of the verandah. Leave nine inches of your verandah floor, then build this little wall eighteen inches high and nine inches wide, and let the top remain nearly flat – not quite flat – us the surface should slope outwards slightly, so that when plants are watered, the waste-water may run off without wetting the floor of the verandah. By this arrangement you can make a great show : one row of flowering plants on the ground, a second row on the 9-inch ledge of the verandah floor, and a third row on the top of the little wall. You will find this a very useful method for keeping things safe from excess of the heat, the rain, and the cold.

Colouring for Pots

There are two kinds of earth very good for this purpose, native names "*Gairoo*" and "*Heermajee.*" These give a rich red colour which enhances the beauty of the plant growing in the pot. Get your coolies to scrub the pots with bits of old rope, or bunches of dried grass. The mali should pound the red earth, mix it with water and rub it on the pots with a rag.

One anna's worth of the coloured earth will colour fifty pots perfectly.

If your plants are valuable, and you wish to keep them as free as possible from insects, use kerosine instead of water for mixing the earth.

Verandah Steps

Coir matting is inexpensive and better than anything I know for covering verandah steps and floors. It lasts for years, white-ants won't touch it, water does not stain it, it can be washed in water, or dust and dirt can be easily shaken from it. It can be obtained from any native firm in India, from three to five annas per square yard. Old coir matting should be chopped up and used as drainage for flower-pots. (*See* "Flower-Pots")

Protection against Vermin

All movable pots, stands, &c., should be moved, and verandahs swept, and afterwards sprinkled with a weak solution of phenyle or kerosine. The smell soon evaporates, but sufficient of its virtue will be retained by the floor, to make it an unwholesome abiding place for flies and insects, to say nothing of toads and snakes!

Avoid having rock-work or creeper-covered *jaffreys* about your verandahs and porches : the former harbours vermin, and the latter obstucts ventilation and protects mosquitoes. Baskets of fern, &c., suspended by *wire,* and pots and rustic stands are quite enough to make your verandahs and porches look charming.

Protection agains Frost

If you have delicate plants in the ground likely to suffer on frosty nights, make a simple coop of wire, pin several folds of newspapers over it, and place it over your plants. Newspapers come in very handy for sheltering flowers and plants when you can't afford glass. A railway inspector travelling on his trolley in winter, once having forgotten to take his overcoat with him, utilised some *newspapers* to protect himself from the cold cutting wind, and found them an effectual covering! So don't despise the use of them for your plants.

Baskets for Plants and Flowers

These always look better with handles. Get the common bazaar rush or "coolie" baskets and make your own handles in this way. In the rains when trees have put forth abundance of new branches, gather a number of *long* supple sprays of tamarind, jaman, dodonia, or *mehndee,* or anything that will afford you long slender twigs from three to four feet long. Remove all the leaves, then plait and interlace these twigs, as regularly as possible, to form bands four or five inches wide. Begin at the thick ends and plait downwards to the thin ends, tying in neatly with little bits of fine twine any refractory twigs. When you have done two of these bands, unite them together by overlapping the thin ends and interlacing them together with the help of a little tying. This makes one handle; fasten the thick ends to your baskets *with wire,* and keep the handle at the curve you wish, by tying it across. Put away your baskets till your handles are quite dry, and then remove the twine that kept the handles in proper curve.

Rustic Supports

For table decoration may be made in all sorts of forms with the same kind of twigs just mentioned, and these may be varnished, painted with colours, or gilded with Bessemer's gold paint.

Flower Supports in Vases

I am sure, when arranging long sprays of flowers in wide-mouthed vases, you have often felt exasperated when the sprays, instead of remaining where you placed them, kept falling over the edge of the vase, destroying all the artistic beauty of your arrangement.

You will find the following hint very useful where you wish to exhibit, to every advantage, just a few sprays of something specially beautiful: – Hold the sprays in your left hand, in the position in which you wish them to remain, and with your right hand, secure that pose by coiling round the stems strong, thick, white, bonnet wire. When this is done, don't cut off the end of the wire, but bend it so as to make it into a star of four or five points radiating from the little tight coil round the flower stems; each point should be just long enough to touch the inner side of the vase, so as to wedge and keep your flowers exactly in the centre.

When you see the success of this arrangement, you will find that, by other judicious bending of this bonnet wire, you will be able to secure for your flowers the most natural appearance you can desire.

Dry the wet wire in the sun after your flowers have faded, and use again.

Varnish for Rustic Work

One quart of methylated spirit, one chittack (2 ozs.) of shellac, sold in the bazaar as *chuppra lac.* Pour off half the spirit into an empty quart-bottle; pound the shellac to a fine powder and put one ounce of it into each of your spirit bottles. Shake well, and keep in the sun for two or three days, and shake occasionally till the lac is dissolved; apply quickly with a brush. The above makes a good varnish for furniture and should be applied with pieces of flannel. (*See* "Baker & Cook")

The same, made a little thinner with half a pint more of spirit, and applied with a brush, will keep *brass* flower-pots and flower-vases a nice, soft, old-gold colour. Applied to copper, it will prevent verdigris.

Coral Varnish

For rustic work may be made in the same way, using red sealing-wax instead of shellac.

Delicate Cuttings

May be induced to root in this way. Take a tumblerful of cotton-wool that is perfectly clean, wet it thoroughly so that it may fill only half the glass : no more water should be in the glass than the wool can absorb. Let the *stems* of your cuttings be completely shrouded in the wet cotton-wool, leaving the head and leaves uncovered; stand the glass where it will get air and light. In a week or ten days, you will find your cuttings have thrown out roots, and may then be planted out in appropriate soil.

– *"Popular Gardener".*

Insects on Plants

Can be got rid of by sponging the leaves with *weak* tobacco water.

– *"The Gardener".*

How to get rid of Insects

Make an emulsion as follows :–

Kerosine	2 gallons	= 66 per cent.
Common Soap	½ lb.	
Water	1 gallon	= 33 per cent.

Heat the solution of soap and add it, boiling hot, to the kerosine. Churn the mixture by means of a force-pump and spray nozzl for five or ten minutes. This emulsion, if perfect, forms a cream upon cooling, and should adhere without oiliness to the surface of glass. *Dilute before using – one part of the emulsion with nine parts of cold water.* The above formula gives three gallons of emulsion, and makes, when diluted, 30 gallons of wash. The same substance will be of great use on hop vines, &c., and will also kill the lice on chickens. It should be sprayed about pretty thoroughly in the hennery.

– *Professor Howard, Entomologist.*

Caterpillars

Don't like crawling through ashes, which should be sprinkled on the surface of the soil and round the stems of plants in pots.

All sorts of Insect Pests

Object to the following remedy :-

Cigar ends should be chopped up, and kept in a jar; take pieces of coarse brown paper, six inches wide and ten inches long, dissolve a table-spoonful of salpetre in a pint of water, dip your papers in the solution, dry them, and keep till wanted. To fumigate, roll one of the pieces of paper into a tube like a cigar, leaving the hollow half-an-inch in diametre, which fill with your chopped cigar ends. Twist one end and stick it into the soil, light the other, and it will burn gradually for an hour or more.

– *"Gardener's Receipt Book".*

Artificial Coral

Take four parts of yellow resin, and one part of vermilion, and melt them together; dip twigs, cinders or stones in this mixture, and it will give them the appearance of coral, and be applicable to rock-work, grotto, or any fancy-work, as a substitute for that costly article.

– *"Gardener's Receipt Book".*

Dried Grasses

For bouquets should be collected towards the end of the rains, both in the hills and plains. Cut them with stalks as long as possible, and tie them up in small bunches, so as to give them plenty of scope to expand and curve naturally and gracefully. Hang up half of your number of bunches, head downwards, and the other half stick in empty quart bottles so that they may curve over. Wire some of them when quite dry, so that you may be able to bend these grasses into position when forming your bouquets.

After the rains, Indian corn is in fine flower. Ask your mali or any servant to buy you a sheaf from a neighbouring field. *"Bhoota ka phool"* is what they call it. The scent is strong like honey, and its plume of shining yellow seeds makes it a very pretty variety for dried bouquets. Stand these in bottles till they are quite dry. Can be used with poppies and cornflowers.

The wire I have advised you to get for horticultural purposes is very good for wiring the stems of your grasses, if you wish your bouquets to be four or five feet high; this wire may be tied to your grass with split fawn-coloured Berlin wool. Whenever you tie it, clip the ends of the wool short.

To Bronze or Colour Grass

Artists' colour-men sell packets of mineral colours in powder. Bronze, green and red are very nice for colouring grasses. Pour a little of the shellac varnish into a small cup or tin, and add enough of the powder you choose, to make it just thick enough to apply to your grasses with a bristle brush; an old paint brush will do, as you won't be able to use it for any other purpose afterwards. Do this painting as quickly as you can, for the varnish evaporates very fast.

The fine seed grass you see growing everywhere in the rains, bronzed in this way and put away, is very useful for bouquets of *fresh* flowers too.

To destroy Maggots and Worms

Roses are attacked in the winter, and coleus, &c., in the rains, by these detestable creatures that are able to destroy an entire plant in a night. The following recipe from the "Gardener's Receipt Book" is a very good preventive against the ravages of these rapacious vermin : – One bushel of unslaked lime in powder, half a pound of sulphur in powder, mix these together dry, then add as much water as will make it almost as thick as honey, boil for an hour, then add half a pound of finely powdered charcoal, mix well together, then apply to the stem of the plant attacked, brushing from below upwards. Wherever you see young leaves coiled up, you will find a maggot, and if there is one, there are sure to be more, so apply your remedy freely. (*See* "Coleus")

Labels

Clean a sheet of zinc : part of the lining of an old box will do. Get your tinman to cut it into slips four inches long and one inch wide, boring a small hole at one end of them, into which insert a small piece of wire by which you may attach them to your shrubs. The following ink, recommended by Mr. W. Jones, can be made by any chemist, and is perfect for writing on zinc :–"Take one drachm of verdigris, one drachm of sal ammoniac powder, and half a drachm of lamp-black, and mix with ten drachms of water;" another ink is a solution of bichloride of platinum, twelve grains to an ounce. If quill pens wear out too rapidly with this, try the reed pens used by natives. For big lettering on metal wood, pasteboard, canvas, &c., the sixpenny conical indiarubber pen is extremely useful, as with it you can write quite easily, even on a rough surface, with common ink, or the above special inks.

To keep Flowers fresh in the Hot Weather

Is, as every one knows, next to an impossiblity; but as I have found the following plan most efficacious, I can recommend it. Take three yards of your wire netting, cut it into two pieces lengthways, so that you may have two pieces three yards long and eighteen inches wide. Join the two ends of one piece together, so as to form a circle. Stand it upright, so that the *cut edge* should be at the *top,* and across this top fix a piece of split bamboo, cross and re-cross it with three other pieces radiating, so that the top of your wire netting bears a sort of a bamboo wheel with eight spokes. See that each spoke is firmly fixed with wire; make use of the other piece of wire netting in the same way. You now have a pair of *covers* large enough to place over two wash-hand basins filled with flowers. Keep these basins on the *floor* of your bath-room, fill with water, and place in them as many flowers as they will hold; *flowers to be cut in the early morning;* put the wire covers over them, and cover up *entirely* with a sheet or several towels, which must be kept constantly wet all day. At night you will find that the damp cloths, and the shutting out of the intense glare, have kept your flowers beautifully fresh.

If you think the wire covers too tiresome to make or too expensive, you might have bamboo hencoops made, *as open as possible,* of the same dimensions – three feet in diameter and eighteen inches high. All the flower-vases taken off the breadfast table and kept under this wet coop all day will have their contents quite fresh enough to adorn the table again at night for dinner. There is something pitifully depressing in the sight of withered flowers on a dining table.

Dried Ferns

For bouquets should be wired *before* they are dried. Choose long, perfect fronds, if they are meant for the tall bouquets for corners of rooms. Cut a piece of garden wire (already mentioned) eight or nine inches longer than your frond; this should be tied to the rib of the frond with a finer wire. As florist's wire is not to be obtained in India, an excellent substitute can be found by ripping up the *flat bonnet wire* sold at two annas a yard.

If you intend to do any artistic work with flowers, you should always keep by you a few yards of this *flat bonnet wire,* which is composed of three or four strands of fine wire covered with a cotton thread, and it is this fine cotton-covered wire, which you unrip from the flat wire, that you will find invaluabl for tying-up purposes. Well, to return to your fern leaf, tie the garden wire to the rib of your fern with little bits of the fine cotton-covered wire here and there, and snip the wire ends quite short and neat. The moisture from the ferns will rust the wire, so that when your ferns are dry and ready for your bouquets, the wire will be of almost the same colour as the ferns.

The leaves of the *Grevillea robusta,* wired in this way, are a great addition to dried bouquets.

All leaves, when wired, should be put away between *large* sheets of newspaper and kept under heavy boxes, &c., and the papers changed occasionally.

Small, fine ferns, for other decorative purposes, may be dried between blotting-papers.

When your ferns are dry enough to make up into bouquets, arrange them with your grasses, tying them to a strong piece of bamboo long enough or short enough for the jar or vase into which you intend to put your bouquet. Thick cotton thread is good for this final tying, and after your bouquet is formed, and quite complete, damp the tied thread; this damping *shrinks the thread* and makes it contract, so that there is less fear of your dried stems slipping out of place.

Colours for Flower-stands

Two colours, which form very effective backgrounds, are Etruscan pink and celadon. The latter colour, a delicate, pale blue-green tint of the all-precious jade, is a favourite with those true flower-artists, the Japanese. You may make these colours yourself in every variety of shade by mixing the following : – White and light red for Etruscan pink; and white, Prussian blue, with a faint touch of chrome yellow, for celadon. One tin (2 pounds) of Hubbuck's prepared white paint, sold everywhere from Re. 1 to 1-4, will go an immense way in painting your stands. One tube of each of the other colours, Prussian blue, light red and chrome yellow (price 5 annas each), will be sufficient for several tins of Hubbuck's white paint. One paint of turpentine for thinning your paints, cleaning your stands and washing your brushes, will cost 8 annas, and a bristle brush will cost 6 or 8 annas.

Celadon. – Put into a cup a little Prussian blue, then add the smallest particle of chrome yellow (as it is very powerful) and mix, then put in the white paint little by little, until you have got the right shade of celadon.

Etruscan pink. – Put a little of your light red into a cup, and add white paint by degrees till you have got the required shade of pink, *i.e.*, like the inside of various sea-shells.

You can make a variety in these background tints by shading them, that is, by painting the lowest part in the darkest shade of colour, and adding more white as you work up towards the top of your flower-stands. This shaded background is particulalry effective for any floral designs you may afterwards think of painting on your flower-stands.

These floral designs should be in monochrome, I mean in one colour, of various tints; on celadon, paint designs in dark autumn greens only; on Etruscan pink, let your designs be in rich brown tints.

Tea-tables

For soldiers' feasts, for school children's treats, &c., may be made to look much nicer than they generally do by a little attention to the way the flowers are arranged. It cannot possibly be a "treat" to any one to sit down to a table, the decorations of which consist of a few odd tumblers, with a mass of many-coloured flowers crammed in anyhow, with all the stems visible in dirty green or yellow water! No one would ask ladies to send down their best vases to such functions. But a vast difference could be made in the decorations of these tables if a little ingenuity were exercised with the common material always at hand, *i.e.*, white cups and saucers, white and coloured paper, &c. Two pretty suggestions are here given, which may be improved upon in many ways.

One dozen common white cups and saucers, a few sheets of white foolscap or thick white paper, flowers of one colour with foliage, or of two or three well contrasting colours. Cups to be arranged in groups of three, the saucers in groups of four, so that, for one long table, you will have seven groups. Now take your paper and cut twelve strips ten inches by eighteen inches, and treat each in the following manner : pleat, or fold in half-inch folds across the *narrow* width of the paper, so that you may have eighteen pleats in each paper. Pass this folded paper through the handle of a cup, letting the handle come exactly in the middle of it. Catch up two corners of the paper equally so that it forms a fan; the two sides of the paper that now meet in the middle of the fan should be held together by pins which won't show behind the pleats. Your cup will now have something of the appearance of a peacock with spread tail! There will be two corners of your paper resting on the table-cloth; draw these *under* the cup so that the weight of the cup may keep them in position. Put some water in the cup, then arrange your flowers in it. You will be able to do this very easily and effectively, as the paper will form a sort of bouquet-holder. Place these cups three together, with the handles all tuned towards the inside of the circle. The edges of the paper may be scalloped before you begin to pleat it.

Now for the saucers : fill them with wet sand, fringe them with leaves of ipomea, carrot, aristolochia, or anything that will droop over the edge, and put in the same coloured flowers as are in the cups, or if you have white flowers in the cups, put red in the saucers, or *vice-versa.* Arrange the groups of four saucers diamond-wise.

The paper arrangement may sound rather troublesome, but I assure you it can be done in a few minutes, and you will be quite pleased with the result of your handiwork, for the cups, with their bouquet papers, will contrast well with the low groups of saucers placed alternately all down the table, and look pretty enough for any one to sit down to table with pleasure.

Another way : take a square of the pretty poppyred *crepe* paper sold by nearly all respectable shops dealing in English goods, at seven annas per roll of ten feet, twenty inches wide; hold it up in the middle as you would a handkerchief, letting the four corners lie flat on the table-cloth, and place a white tea-cup on each corner, letting the handles turn towards the inner side of the circle close together. Straight down the middle of the table-cloth lay a 9-inch wide strip of the red paper, which may be scalloped at the edge, or bordered with sprays of ipomea. In the centre, have one group of four cups; on either side of this, place six saucers in the red strip of paper, and finish both ends with other groups of four cups. Yellow flowers with brown leaves, or white and yellow flowers (no *green* leaves) make an uncommon effect. The raised point of red paper in the centre of the groups of cups may be dept erect by a small piece of bamboo underneath.

Pretty bright "Turkey red" (*saloo*), sold in the bazaar at 4 annas per yard, may be used instead of paper. White tea-cups and saucers can *always* be hired *everywhere* for a trifle, and you can improve on these two simple ideas in very many ways, and make the tea-tables in your charge look inviting, without expense or risk. The nice things provided for "Treats" and "Feasts" will look all the nicer for their floral settings.

Flowers for Hospitals

Are always acceptable. You will have plenty of flowers in your garden to provide a dozen small bouquets for this purpose, once a week, in turns with othe ladies, who could do so on other days. A clergyman, who kindly took charge of these hospital bouquets, once told me that he always felt "armed with the sweetest weapons of persuasion." Ruskin calls them the "solace of humanity"- and how much more of a solace must the sight of fresh sweet flowers be to *suffering* humanity?

> "To me the meanest flower that blows can give
> Thoughts that do often lie too deep for tears."
>
> – *Wordsworth.*

Flowers in the Hot Weather

Are Amaryllis, Amaltas, Bignonia venusta, Bombax malabaricum, Dodonea, Ixora, kuchnar, Lagestroemia Indica, Mehndee, Plumbago, Russellia, Oleanders, Quisqualis, Tecoma stans, Zephyranthes, &c., & c.

Flowers and Foliage Plants in the Rains

Are Acalyphas, Alternanthera, Amaranthus, Antigonum leptopus (Sandwich Island creeper), Arundo donax, Balsam, Box, Caladiums, Camphire (Mehndee), Coleus, Canna, Cyanotis, Duranta, Hibiscus, Inga dulcis, Ixora, Kuronda, Lilies, Lagestroemia, Oleanders, Pilea muscosa, Plumbago, Quisqualis, Russellia, Teak, Yucca, Zinnias, &c., &c.

Cold-Weather Flowers

Are without number! Annuals of all kinds, Camphire, Cyanotis, Ferns, Honeysuckle, Hollyhocks, Roses, Mina lobata, &c., &c.

Flowers in the Hills

Almost all the annuals that grow on the plains will grow in the hills, besides a great many more English ones that don't grow very well on the plains,– Bignonias, Geraniums, Carnations, Anemones, Dahlias, Asters, Godetia, Myosotis, Narcissus, &c., &c.

Begin your garden work as soon as the cold weather lessens, some time in February, and sow your seeds from March to beginning of May.

Watch your bulbous plants and take them in hand as soon as they *'begin to move.'* Gladiolous, Iris, Amaryllis, Narcissus, &c., first, and all Liliums, later on, from May to September.

Roses. – As you are in the hills usually from April to October, you will naturally wish for as many rose blooms as can be produced during those months, so your best plan will be to give your roses fresh soil and manure in *June before the rains begin,* and then prune them. (*See* Paragraphs "Treatment of Roses" and "Rose Cuttings," &c.) At the June pruning, cut away all old, dry wood.

You will have many blooms during the rains, and if you snip off the *ends* of branches, and mulch the surface of the soil round your roses in the spring at the beginning of *March*, you will, then, have some more good blooms. But remember, at this hot time of year, you must give your roses as much water as you can spare.

Chrysanthemums should be separated in the spring and pinched back if they make too rapid growth in the summer. If the suckers are not separated your flowers will not be good. Manure the roots in September, or as soon as the rains cease, and when the flower-buds begin to form, snip off more than half of them. You will have more plants than you know what to do with, keep the best ones in your front garden, and plant the rest among the dahlias on your hillside along the bank from your gateway, &c., and you will have abundant blooms for cutting.

Heliotropes do splendidly in the hills, becuase the soil, mostly shale, affords the natural drainage necessary for them. Here they will grow from *cuttings,* and from seeds, which may be struck and sown at the end of February. Plant a good many in pots, and place these in raised mounds or banks, because if you have *snow,* these pots can be taken up and sheltered in-doors. Some of the stronger plants, placed against a south wall and protected with dried leaves, will survive in Himalyan hill stations, if the winter is not abnormally severe.

Some of the better kinds you raise from seeds up herè you should take down to the plains, where you can't manage to produce them from seed.

Geraniums and *Bignonias* only need sheltering from heavy rain and snow. Give them powdered charcoal and chopped cocoanut fibre, and increase by cuttings. Keep your better kinds in verandahs; the commoner, hardy ones will grow on raised beds round shady trees. Rooted cuttings should be taken down to the plains, where they will thrive very well from October to March. In fact, Bignonias will thrive in the plains all the year round, especially in rustic "trays" and "hanging baskets," if kept in verandahs where they will get only the morning sun.

Flowers in Southern Stations

The times for seed sowing, pruning, transplanting, etc., in the south of India must naturally be somwhat different from those suitable to Northern Stations.

From my own observations, and from advice in the "Lawrence Asylum Press Almanack," the month of August should mark the beginning of your garden work. Sow the seeds of your annuals. Prune your roses, and plant your cuttings. This is the time to manure and freshen the soil of all rooted plants.

In September plant out your seedlings, trim your hedges, make cuttings of geraniums, carnations, etc., and sow seeds of shrubs and trees.

In October roses, fuschias, violets and all budding plants that are sending out new, vigorious shoots, may be planted out.

In November mulch your roses. If the rains are heavy, protect your delicate plants.

In December late annuals may be planted out, and fresh sowings made of phlox, petunias, &c.

Your flowers ought to be at their best in January. During the hottest time before the rains, take care of your roses, &c.

Prune common, fast-growing roses in Jun and July, re-pot bulbs, and make general preparations for seed sowing.

You must remember that the soils for and methods of treatment, given in this book, apply to flowers and their culture all over India, and that it is *the time for gardening operations that varies.*

Arrangements of Flowers

Pray remember these are mere *hints* for you to improve upon, and I give them because, especially in the hot weather and the rains, everyone does not know what floral treasures are available, and what would be the most effective method of arrangement. Let me advise your having by you, for a small and for a long table, one piece of Pongee silk a yard square, and another three yards long, both in the following colours :– pale-blue, pale-pink apricot, eau-de-nil of a very light shade, and a light poppy-red (that charming red you always see in Japanese lacquer work). The colours I have mentioned can be obtained in a good kind of *satin* made at Azamgurh, N.W.P. : it is thirty-six inches wide, and sold at Re. 1-6 per yard, which is very nice for table use.

Economy being the order of the present day, I say nothing about your vases and flowe receptacles. The incomparable beauty and effect of exquisite Royal Worcester-ware, of chased silver bowls, and of priceless old China 'goes without saying,' but you and I may not posess these, so we will arrange the flowers which we *do* possess, in the most artistic way and to the greatest advantage. Pictures without frames, hung on bare white walls, do not appear to advantage, so that is why I advise the purchase of the above-mentioned silks or satins, they are the *frames* in which your flowers will look their best on your white table-cloths.

Amaltas, another boon in the hot weather, always looks best without any foliage; but if you would prefer some garniture, the *bronze grasses* are what will suit best. The amaltas arranged in waves of the red silk recommended, has an imposing Venetian effect of colouring. The only other coloured silk you can use with amaltas is the pale-blue, in which case omit the bronzed grass and use cyanotis.

Amaranthus melancholicus ruber makes a very good hall decoration at the beginning of the hot weather, arranged with masses of what do you think? The white flowers of the common radish, or the yellow flowers of the humble mustard! Your mali is sure to have plenty he is keeping for seed, and the blooms will give you elegant decorations, if you are not too fastidious.

Amaryllis. – Cut these in the morning and keep under your damp 'coop' if you wish to use them at night. When these lilies are in bloom, the mango trees will be putting out their new leaves. Gather some of these for the garniture of your lilies; if you don't use these new brown leaves, arrange them with sprays of *Arando donax* instead. In either case, pale-blue or eau-de-nil silk will suit for the 'setting'.

Balsams can only be used for low decorations. Saucers of wet sand will keep the blossoms stuck in them quite fresh for twenty-four hours. Bright red balsams, also the coral pink ones, make a very pretty dining-table decoration framed in pale-blue or apricot-coloured silk. If you have mirror plaques, a very effective way of using them is as follows : – Cut a piece of American glazed cloth one or two inches wider than your plaque all round, put a false hem to it one inch wide of some pink cambric or sateen and draw a string through the hem, tightening it just enough to turn up the edges. (The hem should be on the unvarnished side of the cloth.) When you turn up the edge, the *varnished side* must be *inside* the bag: fill with wet sand and place on your pale-blue silk, fix an inverted saucer or soup-plate (according to the size of yiour bag) in the middle, and bank up the sand round the edge as high as you can. Then place your mirror plaque on the top of the sand heap and fill up the space between the silk and the plaque with dark-red or pink balsams, stuck in the wet sand. You have no idea till you try, how very uncommon and striking these mounds of balsams are, the higher the better with the mirror plaques on the top. On the mirror plaques place your vases or bowls filled with foliage only, ferns, grasses, acalypha, amaranthus, &c., &c., all flourishing during the rains.

(The American cloth bags serve for other arrangements. They should be wiped dry after using.)

Bignonia venusta is too decided a colour for a dining-table, but a large bowl of it on your side-board and one of your long-handled wicker baskets filled with it in your drawing-room, will be very striking.

Bombax malabaricum does not admit of being cut in long sprays, so a *low* set of flower-stands will suit it best, even soup-plates of wet sand fringed with cyanotis will do. Apricot-coloured silk harmonizes beautifully with this lovely jungle-flower. This arangement also suits another jungle tree flower the *Butea frondosa* (native name *Dhak*), which is in flower in the hot weather.

Cyanotis lasts a long time if kept moist. It is a most useful garniture, and must always be dipped into water before using. It can be *wired* for many purposes :– arches for dinner-tables, nests for saucers filled with flowers, bordering for rustic table decoration, such as you will find described in paragraphs "Sweet-pea" and "Verbenas." &c., &c.

Dodonea, the pale, apple-green flowers of which are in profusion in the hot weather, will afford you many refreshing combinations of tints, as it looks well with white and with pink oleanders; with white *Ixora*, and with *Tecoma stans*, all obtainable at the same time. Eau-de-nil silk should be used with dodonea and white oleanders, also with dodonea and white ixora; dodonea mixed with pink oleanders, pink silk; and with *Tecoma stans* and dodonea use apricot silk or satin. Dodonea keeps fresh for several days. Red *Ixora* (only flowers, no leaves) looks particularly well with pale-blue silk.

Hollyhocks are most useful flowers for wiring when you want a large show. Cut them *just before using*, and wire in the same way as "Yucca gloriosa"; arrange double pink hollyhocks with the teak blossoms, or Gypsophila; the lemon-coloured with Arundo donax and *mehndee;* the deep red hollyhocks with dark foliage. Hollyhocks sometimes appear self-sown in the rains, and last through the cold months, so you will have many varieties of effects with them. They are very effective in tall stands and baskets for hall and drawing-room decorations.

Kuchnar, white, is one of the most delightful flowers to arrange, for whatever you may combine with it, you are sure to be pleased with the result. Nestling with camphire in billows of pale-blue, or eau-de-nil silk; arranged with *pilea muscosa,* or with ferns in soft pink silk; and by itself in red silk, the kuchnar is always lovely.

Lagestroemia indica, white, like sea-foam, you can revel in, both during the hot weather and rains. Elegant and graceful in itself, a few sprays of Arundo donax is all it needs, and framed in pale-blue or eau-de-nil is the most refreshing sight your eye can rest upon, in the way of a dinner table, on a hot evening. A mass of pink *lagestroemia* in your long-handled baskets, with the new leaves of the jaman, or of acalypha, is splendid for drawing-room decoration.

Oleanders are a great resource in both hot weather and rains. White oleander with dodonea, and pale-blue or eau-de-nil silk for a frame, is very cool-looking for a dinner-table in the hot weather. With grasses (its own leaves are too stiff) or ferns in the rains, it is exquisite, surrounded with soft pink sild. The pink oleander with *amaranthus ruber,* coleus, also with acalypha foliage, is lovely, arranged with pale-blue silk, or with pink silk for the dining-table, and in large masses in tall flowerstands for drawing-rooms, &c., &c.

Orchids and *Lilies,* so plentiful in the hills during the hot weather and rains, are made doubly effective by the use of mirrors, in plaques or strips. If moss is placed for bedding them, use the "American cloth" bags, in long or round forms, to guard against the wetting of table-coths. In paragraph "Crystallised Grasses and Stands", you will find an idea that greatly enhances the effect of flowers on mirrors.

Phlox, which is in flower through the cold months and well into the hot weather, gives you charming low decorations for the dining-table. Arrange in saucers with wet sand or moss; fringe with maiden-hair fern, or with selaginella mutabilis, filling the centre with red, pink or white phlox.

Plumbago, which you will have plenty of during the hot weather and rains, looks very well by itself in white china, or mixed with gypsophila in tall vases. A large mass of this elegant bloom, arranged in wicker-baskets painted dark green or bright red, gives a delightful touch of colour in a drawing-room, especially if, to the long handle of the green or red basket, you tie a large ribbon bow of corresponding colour.

Quisqualis, the dear quisqualis, is a treasure in both hot weather and rains. Gather the flowers in the morning and arrange for your breakfast-table, then remove to the protecting "cooop" till dinner-time in the hot weather. This protection will not be needed in the rains Quisqualis, with camphire, is a sweet combination. If wanted *specially* for evening use, gather in the morning, and keep under the 'coop'; by four or five o'clock in the afternoon, you will find the sweet pale-pink buds all open; leave all the pale-pink blossoms on the stems, but remove all the dark-red ones. Mix the pale-pink sprays with camphire in your vases (*no leaves*), and stick the dark-red flowers in saucers, filled with wet sand and fringed with alternanthera. This arrangement looks sweet and uncommon, framed in pink, blue, or apricot silk. The puffs of silk should rise well up to the edge of the saucers, which should be placed all round a large, pale-pink centre, or between a series of small vases filled with the pale-pink sprays. Quisqualis looks equally well arranged with teak blossoms, which are abundant in the rains.

For drawing-room use, long sprays of quisqualis need some support, and torch-like effects can be obtained by taking three or four sprays of equal length and wiring them to a piece of bamboo, taking care not to allow this bamboo support to be seen, and to let the stems lie well in water below.

Russellia juncea with white oleanders, or white zephyranthes, is a pleasing variety. *Russellia floribunda* with yellow zinnias, or with *Tecoma stans* (without any green leaves), looks charming in low masss with apricot silk for the dining table, and with a foundation of alternanthera in baskets for the drawing-room during the rains.

Sandwich Island creeper, Antigonum leptopus, is chamingly arranged in the same way as balsams, with pale-blue silk surroundings; but in the vases put the same flowers, no foliage except the bronzed grasses.

For the drawing and other rooms this pretty pink Antigonum is effective in hanging baskets, its own bright green leaves allowed to remain, or removed, and cyanotis ("Wandering Jew") mixed intstead. Masses of it on mantel-pieces, banked with cyanotis (on wet sand in long flat American cloth bags) are very showy on festive occasions.

Tecoma stans mixed with pink oleanders, no foliage whatever, gives a rich uncommon effect, set in a frame of apricot silk. A very pretty variety of arrangement in the hot weather.

Zephyranthes, if wanted for night use, should be cut in the morning when half open, and the stems placed in very wet sand under the damp "coop". If used for drawing-room, place in vases that will hold wet sand, or fill a large flat tin with wet sand and fit it into a basket, cover over the sandy surface with cyanotis or ipomea, and stick our zephyranthes, pink or white, all over between the leaves. Very pretty and effective.

Wedding Cake Decorations

For these purposes the white duranta is particularly well suited; its small sprays, cut away from the large stems and wired, can be fixed round the bottom of the cake in a lovely drooping fringe. Of course you will use whatever white flowers are available according to the time of year, but if gypsophila and alliums are to be had, you will find nothing so *graceful* as garniture for your larger flowers. As the cake is the special ambrosia furnished for the Hymeneal feast, every one is anxious it should be placed in a specially and conspicuously attractive way. Let me suggest one which was greatly admired. Choose a moderate sized *round* table and make a large cushion for the top of it in this way :– Cut two circles of coarse white calico six or seven inches, smaller in diameter than the top of the table. Sew the two edges of the circles together; in the centre of them cut a hole, the diameter of which must be a *little smaller* than the size of the cake; take a strip of the same kind of calico, twelve inches wide, and join it along the edge of the hole to *one* of the circles, then join the other side of the strip to the other circle. This will form a shape like a huge *Air-cushion,* only air-cushions when not distended with air lie perfectly flat; but your calico cushion must stand twelve inches high in the middle, owing to the 12-inch strip of calico forming, as it were, a hollow tube in the centre. Fill your cushion with bran, sawdust, coir, or dry hemp, spread your damask table-cloth on the round table, and place your cushion in the middle; in the hole of the cushion place a round tin box, or anything firm and high enough to support the cake. On the space between the edge of the cushion and the margin of the table lay a flat fringe of ferns, cover *all* the surface of the cushion with fresh green moss, and then fix your white flowers in the moss with hair-pins, which running easily into the sawdust or hemp of the cushion, will hold them in place securely.

The above arrangement can be varied by having your cushion made in scallops, and if fresh green velvety moss is not procurable, then throw a long piece of satin or silk over the cushion, seeing that it is long enough and wide enough to admit of its being pinched up in graceful puffs. Use silk or satin of the palest chartreuse, or apple-green tint, which willmake the darker green leaves of your white flowers stand out with greater effect. Large white stain ribbon bows here and there will eke out the flowers. Avoid an all-white foundation; it is monotonous and does not display the cake as well as the moss or green silk does. (*See* "Crystallised Grasses," &c)

Stains on Flower Vases

Of glass and china, if of long standing, can be removed by the use of a weak solution of hydrochloric acid, obtainable from all chemists. Don't touch this acid with your fingers, but apply it with a bit of rag tied firmly to the end of a small stick; rub the stains well, then wash your vases in lukewarm water, and dry with clean cloths. After your vases are thus perfectly free from stains, half a small lemon should always be kept on he mali's flower-tray. If this piece of lemon is rubbed daily on the stains that rare naturally caused by the water and flowers, your vases will look as good as new, though used for years. When lemons are not to be had a little vinegar will do as well.

To keep Cut Flowers Fresh

There are various ways :– Putting a teaspoonful of powdered charcoal into the water of the vase in which your flowers are placed; leaving them out of doors in the dew all night; when you snip the ends off flower stems, hold the stem *under water*, and don't let the air get to the freshly cut stem. Flowers meant to be worn can be kept fresh by wrapping narrow strips of gutta-percha or oiled silk, round the tips of the stems, so as to exculde the air. Flowers last longer if cut in the morning; if cut during the day, their vitality is weakened by rapid evaporation.

To Pack Flowers for Travelling

If they are to accompany you, the following plan will be found excellent : – Place the flowers close together in a large bowl or basin, with sufficient water to keep the stems immersed to a depth of four inches. Sink the bowl in a basket, the sides of which should rise at least six inches above the surface of the flowers. Stretch a cotton cloth over the basket, and tie firmly round the edge. If you keep this cloth moist during your journey you will find your flowers are perfectly fresh when you remove the cloth. The great thing is to keep off all dust, and let the air that reaches them through the cloth be quite damp. If the *cloth* is allowed *to rest in contact with the flowers,* all the tips of the petals will be found decayed and the colours spoiled, so for a *long journey* see that there is a space f six inches between the flowers and their damp covering.

If water in the bowls cannot be managed, soft cotton-wool wrapped round the ends of the stems and kept *quite moist* will answer nearly as well.

Cut Flowers sent as Railway Parcels

Will travel very well if packed as follows :– Scop a raw potato, and place in the hole as many stems of your flowers as it will hold, and then wrap both potato and stems in *wet cotton-wool.* Make as many bouquets in this way as you can place upright in your box, arrange so that they can't tumble about. Stretch a thin cotton cloth over the flowers, and nail to the sides of your box, quite taut, so that if the box is turned upside down, the flowers may come in contact with the soft cloth, and not against the hard lid. *This cloth should be dry,* and nailed just one inch above the surface of the flowers. Choose a box deep enough to admit of four or five inches of space between the cloth and the lid of the box, which should be nailed down securely.

For a short railway journey tie your flowers in a large bouquet, wrap wet cotton-wool round the stems, put a dry handkerchief all over the bouquet, and tie the whole *upright in a basket with a cover.*

If the cotton-wool is thoroughly wet, the flowers will travel quite safely for twelve hours. (*See* "Chrysanthemums")

For a long railway journey, say, thirty-six hours in the cold weather, take a deal-wood box about a foot deep, without a cover, nail narrow strips of deal-wood a foot long and two inches wide, one in each corner of the box, and then fasten other strips across to form a frame like that which we use on our bedsteads for supporting mosquito nets.

Spread thick cotton cloth *inside* the box and bring the corners of the cloth over the sides of the box, and put a layer of cotton-wool over the bottom. Now tie your flowers in small bunches, wrap the stems in cotton-wool, and pack them *closely in an upright position* in the box. The bunches should be placed near each other so as to be quite compact, and the cotton-wool should be wetted profusely.

After you have placed in the box as many flowers as it will hold, draw the corners of the cloth up over the transverse strips of wood, envelope-fashion, and sew them up, so that no part is left open. Water this cloth *all over,* nail the address to the side of the box, and despatch it at once. Flowers which I have sent my friends in this way, reached them delightfully fresh.

If you are in the hills, use moss instead of cotton-wool for packing geraniums, dahlias, and such flowers as your amateur friends in the plains can't very well cultivate.

To Crystallise Grasses, Stands, &c

Break up into small bits half a pound of alum and put it into a pan which should be rather flat, or very deep, so as to admit of your grasses being laid, or held in it. Pour a seer, or little more, of *boiling water* on the broken alum and stir till it is dissolved. Hold your grasses in the solution, a few at a time, and deep moving them gently, so that small crystals should form. Very large crystals would form if the solution were not kept disturbed all the time your grasses were in it.

As the water cools, you will see what degree of crystallisation your grasses have attained, if not enough, take them out, put the pan on the fire, and as soon as the alum has dissolved, give your grasses another dipping.

Hang up your sprays to dry, and those you wish to have a curved or drooping from, place in empty quart bottles till dry.

You can make very pretty rustic supports for flowers by pinching wire into shapes, covering them thickly with cotton-wool and thread, and then dipping them into the solution. Suspend the shapes by a thread to a piece of stick, and shake it gently all the time till ready. These are very pretty when used for flowers in connection with mirrors.

The addition of Judson's dyes, just a few drops to the plain alum solution, will give you any colour you like in crystals.

To Frost Foliage, &c

The prettiest effect in frosting can be obtained by the use of powdered *Talc* (native name "*abrook*"), very cheap and easily procured in every bazaar. Proceed as follows : – See that your talc is free from all dirty specks, and then pound it to a fine powder; put one teaspoonful of perfectly clean liquid gum into a teacupful of hot water, and mit it well. Have all the sprays of foliage you are going to frost brushed free from all dust, withered bits, &c., then lay them on sheets of newspaper, and with an old tooth-brush and a comb "splutter" them with the weak solution of gum; each time you dip the brush into the cup, press it against the side, so as not to take up too much liquid. When you have "spluttered" all your sprays, remove them to other clean, dry sheets of newpapers, and before the gum drieds, sprinkle them all over with the powdered talc.

Let the sprays remain where they are for about a quarter of an hour, then take them up, giving each a gentle fillip with the finger to free them from the loose talc, which, falling on dry newspapers, can be gathered up and used for other sprays.

Scent Sachets

Are not difficult to make. Snip off blossoms of honey suckle, jasmine, violets, mignonette, &c., dust them over thickly with very dry arrowroot, fold them up in tissue paper and place the packets in envelopes. Use *fresh*, not dried flowers, separately, or mixed together.

For Christmas Decorations

Tiny bits of white cotton-wool should be stuck on the foliage here and there before the gum is "spluttered" and the talc is sprinkled. In frosting "Christmas Trees" the same process on a larger scale will answer, only the powdered talc should be taken up on bits of paper, and *blown* on to the tree.

Sprays of dry grass and wired fern leaves with the powdered talc *blown* on them form very pretty church decorations at Christmas. (*See* "Immortelles,"&c)

Caladiums

In pots used for in-door decoration should always be put out of doors into the open air at night and changed frequently else the leaves will begin to droop. Cut leaves with keep fresh for a long time if there is an inch or two of sand in the water in which they are placed.

Coleus

Sprays and even the leaves by themselves last a long time placed in wet sand. You will have plenty during the rains, and those which you have cut up and planted in the ground after the rains, will afford you much foliage by Christmas, to use with your chrysanthemums.

Gardenia

(The name usually given for convenience to *Taberna montana coronaria)* will provide you with exquisite flowers almost all the year round, but especially in the rains. When cut, don't sprinkle water *on* them, since damp stains the petals, and if you wish them to remain fresh and pure as long as possible, *dry* the blossoms with an old soft pocket handkerchief. If you change the water every day, snip off the end of the stems, and cut away the faded, full-blown flowers, the clusters of buds will remain fresh and serviceable for many days, and when arranged with green grass and *pilea muscosa,* form a most refreshing sight.

Hibiscus

The kind you have been advised to cultivate, are best by themselves; their beauty does not require the support of other flowers. If required for decorations by lamp-light, gather them in the morning and keep under the damp coop all day.

H. Rosa Sinensis

In tall, pale-green vases, or arranged in low baskets or stands in folds of *eau-de-nil* silk is a glorious sight.

Honeysuckle

Sprays when cut for in-door use should have their stems placed in a good depth of water, so put them in rather tall vases, and if you change the water every day and snip the stems, the clusters of buds will continue to open quite to the end of the sprays, a virtue not possessed by all flowers.

Canna

For in-door use cut the sprays in long lengths and place in wet sand, which, if freshened up every day with additional moisture, will keep your canna good for a long time. Your black and gold kerosine tins (mentioned elsewhere) will be very useful filled with long sprays of canna to decorate verandahs, &c. It is also effective for stage decoration.

Chrysanthemums

Flower in thick, close bunches, and one does not like cutting off sprays on which there are still many half-opened buds; but fortunately, cut chrysanthemums last a good while : so when you cut off the full-blown flowers, wire their short stems and wrap them in wet cotton-wool. For table decoration they look exquisie on fresh moss or mirrors. Strips of mirror five or six inches wide laid all round the edge of any of the coloured silks advised, and fringed with cut white chrysanthemums on one side and frosted foliage on the other is truly fairy-like. The inner edge of the glass, next the silk, should be tilted up a little by placing small balls of crushed paper under the silk. If yellow or red chrysanthemums are used in this way, substitute the bronze coleus leaves for frosted foliage. In the angles formed at the corners of the strips of glass place clusters of chrysanthemums in small low glasses.

Chrysanthemums flower abundantly in the hills long before they appear in the plains and may be packed for trvelling in the following manner : – Line your box with soft calico, place a layer of flowers on the bottom, hammer a nail about one and a-half inch long into each side of the box just above the surface of your flowers, make frames of light strips of bamboo, or strong wire to fit the inside of your box exactly, stretch pieces of cotton cloth tightly across, and lay them in the box so as to be supported by the nails. Continue these layers of flowers on the frames till your box is full, spread a piece of calico on the top, then nail down the lid. Chrysanthemums packed this way will bear a thirty-six hours' journey in the cold weather quite safely. *All the calico used must be dry.* (*See* "Yucca")

Immortelles or Everlastings

Can be used effectively in dried bouquets. Can be bronzed with the mineral powders recommended, and are extremely useful frosted over for Christmas decorations.

Inga dulcis

Recommended for hedges, has a peculiar bloom after the rains, which makes it a desirable foliage for many purposes : borders for slips, handles for baskets garlands for walls, & c., &c.; dip into water before using.

Jasminum syringafolium

Is most useful for Easter decorations. It should be cut overnight and kept under the damp coop; the open blossoms will have fallen off by the morning, but the buds will gradually expand and remain on their stems for a longer time than they would if they opened in the sunlight.

Jasminum officinale

Should be gathered in the morning; its buds open in the evening and perfume the whole house deliciously. When cutting this flower, choose sprays with white-looking *buds*, which are very pretty by themselves or as a garniture for roses, &c.

Marguerites

Are pretty enough for a hundred different kinds of arrangements, so I will suggest only one or two which I found particularly effective. Yellow marguerites with mignonette, brown leaves, and bronzed grass, nestling in pale *eau-de-nil* silk; white marguerites with poppies and corn are very nice in sheafs supported by red paper rosettes, for decorating *tea-tables* already mentioned.

Mina lobata

Charming by itself, looks more effective if used in combination with nasturtiums. For a dining-table use it in the taller stand with bronzed grasses, and nasturtiums in the lower ones. *M. lobata* will remain fresh for a week after it is cut.

Mirrors, Coloured Glass, &c

The prettiest adjuncts in floral decorations can be obtained at most reasonable prices in India. Mirror plaques in different sizes at the Army and Navey Cooperative Society, Apolo Street, Bombay. Mirror glass in all sorts of widths and lengths can be bought at wonderfully chep rates from Hurjee Sajoon, looking-glass merchant, No. 66, Khalasee Chuckla, Bombay. Strips of mirror recommended for chrysanthemums, &c., can be had from him at four annas per strip, and he will cut the glass for jardinieres, &c., in any shape you like.

Coloured glass will be supplied to you at a very small cost by Messrs. Netroo Lall Day & Co., No. 1, Old Court House Lane, Calcutta.

Moss Baskets

For these bend pieces of your *wire netting* into any shape you like, tying and fixing with wire, and then covering the whole with brown or green calico. On shapes like these you can easily *sew* on the moss, beginning at the bottom, finish at the edge of the brim, with a narrow layer of additional moss, like a small *rouleau.* Instead of saturating your moss baskets with water put them out in the dew at night, when you will find the lace-like films expand naturally. If this cannot be done, a *very* wet cloth kept on the surface of the moss all night, is the next best method of freshening the baskets.

Nasturtiums

Look best without their own leaves. Almost all the shades harmonize well with apricot silk for a frame, and cyanotis as garniture. (See "*Mina lobata*")

Pansies

You will find when your pansies are in bloom there will be more of purple and mauve than of black or yellow. When painting your flower-stands in celadon tints, do up two or three small wicker-baskets in the same colour, to put your pansies in. You will find an all-mauve-arrangement of flowers in these celadon-coloured baskets extemely pretty. The Nymph in Drayton's *"Muses Elysium"* says–

"The pretty pansy then I'll tye,
Like gems some chain inchasing;
And next to them, their near ally,
The purple violet placing".

And you might go a little further and use heliotrope too, which will be in abundant bloom at the same time as your pansies and violets. (*See* "Violets")

Petunias

(White) form a sweet and graceful in-door decoration. Cut rather long sprays and arrange them with *Arundo donax* and green grasses in tall stands and large baskets.

Phlox

"The indispensable phlox," as Firminger calls, it, makes a lovely table decoration by itself. The petals are too fragile to bear being mixed with other flowers. Fill saucers with wet sand, and place all-pink, all-white or all-red phlox in them without greenery of any kind, and sink these saucers into billows of silk on your dining-table, having other flowers of the same tint in tall glasses. Have pale apple-green silk for pink phlox, pale-blue silk for red or white phlox. The foregoing is one of the prettiest changes you can have, phlox having a particularly soft and delicate effect.

Poppies

You will, of course, put with your cornflowers and wheat-ears in different vases, but if you will put only red poppies and wheat-ears (no cornflowers) in your celadon-tinted flower-stands, you will be delighted with the effect. Poppies with yellow *bhoota* (Indian corn) sprays on *eau-de-nil* silk make a very uncommon and pretty table decoration. (*See* "Plumbago")

Roses

In the arrangement of these it seems really presumptuous to offer any hints! The queen of flowers needs nothing beyond her own foliage, and somtimes, in the case of drooping roses like *Elise Sauvage,* al little garniture, such as mignonette, gypsophila, camphire and ferns; *malis do not understand this,* and invariably spoil the perfect beauty of the rose by arranging with it other flowers of all sizes and shades of colour. Let me implore you to give your mali a lesson or two in treating the rose with proper feeling!

Sweet-pea

Looks well in masses placed in large baskets and tall flower-stands kept near open doors or windows, so that air passing over them may perfume your rooms. I have advised your having plenty and to spare, as this is a flower particularly well suited for hospital bouquets. The purple sweet-pea looks best by daylight; the pink sweet-pea best by lamp-light.

If you have got ready some of the *rustic supports* recommended, sweet-pea, arranged as follows, will afford you a charming variety for table decoration : – Twigs plaited into bands four or fine inches wide and gilded, and also into circles of the same width, will now come into use. For a long table lay your pale-pink sild (or pale-blue) in soft puffs down the centre; place narrow long bags of American cloth all round the edge and fill with wet sand. (Catch the edges of these bags together with long safety-pins here and there to prevent their gaping.) Now put your pink sweet-peas into the wet sand, bank them up on the outer side with the bands of gilded twigs, and on the inner side draw up the silk to the edge of the bags. If you have done any grasses with green mineral powder, you can vary the effect by using *eau-de-nil* silk and the shining green grass with pink swet-pea.

Sumatra Box

Which is in lovely bloom during the rains is most useful for bridal decorations. It is sweet scented, and lasts a long time after it is cut. Its own glossy leaves contrast well with the white blossoms and are abundant enough to afford foliage for other kinds of flowers.

Teak-Tree Blossoms

Which appear in the rains will give you much help as flower garniture. Tea-roses, of which you will have plenty in the rains, look lovely nestling in the fine cream-coloured network of the *teak* blossoms. Quisqualis also goes well with this pretty wild garniture.

Tradescantia

Is most useful for fire-places, stage scenery, &c. Plunge the entire head of your sprays into water to wash off all dust, and then stick the stem into the wet sand with which your pots, bags, or boxes must be filled. It will keep fresh for many days in this way.

Verbenas

Like phlox are best arranged by themselves. In large baskets lined with tin to hold wet sand, the surface covered with alternanthera or moss, put your white, pink and deep red verbenas. Your long bags of American cloth will hold them beautifully to fringe the edge of your dining-table silks; to border your mantel-piece, &c., either in single or mixed colours.

Violets

Having fragile stems are not easy to arrange in large masses, so give your mali a ball of basting cotton, and let him prepare them for your purposes by tying them up in tiny bunches, ten or twelve violets round one piece of mignonette, or nestling in the hollow of single violet leaves. Baskets, tin-lined, and filled with very wet sand, may hold masses of your violets done up in the tiny bunches, the longer stronger stems of mignonette helping the suction and keeping them fresh for a longer time. When heliotrope and purple pansies are added to your violets they will afford intoxicating delight.

Nothing is more suited for hospital bouquets than violets.

Yucca gloriosa

Will, as its name implies, afford you *glorious* decorations in the rains. For large flower-stands the short sprays will have to be wired and the stems wrapped round with a little cotton-wool which will draw up moisture sufficient to keep them fresh, from the water in the vases which the stems themselves are too short to reach. *Arundo donax*, and broad brades of green grass, set off these lovely white bells beautifully, and your poppy-red silk will show them up better than any other colour.

For low decorations, use the bells separately, turning back the petals, when they will look like the eucharis lily. When you intend to use them in this way, cut the bells off the stems, and lay them on a dry towel *for a couple of hours before you turn back the petals,* else the crisp, fresh petals will crack under this operation. These open bells look extremely well laid on your red silk, on dishes of moss, on baskets full of alternanthera, &c., &c. If reuired for travelling, gently wipe the open petals with a soft handkerchief, so as to remove any surface moisture, and lay them between the calico frames advised for chrysanthemum boxes. Packed in this way they will bear a journey of twenty-four hours quite well; see that the petals are not cracked when you turn them back.

Zinnias

Have the virtue of remaining fresh when cut for a longer time than most flowers. As they have no foliage of their own to use with them 'as cut flowers,' arrange them with leaves of *millingtonia* (cork tree), *jaman, tecoma stans,* &c. I know no flower that sets off a hall or corridor as well as the zinnia does, when arranged in masses with the above foliage. *Avoid the pink and magenta colours,* and use only those in shades of yellow, orange and dark red. Put some sand into the water, and if you renew the foliage every day, your zinnias will brighten your hall for many days and prove quite a boon, becuase they are at their best just when you have very little of any other flowers in your garden.

> "If thou wouldest attain to thy highest, go look upon a flower; what that does willessly, that do thou willingly".
>
> –*Schiller.*

"Sic Vos Non Vobis". – Virgil

INDEX

A

Acalypha Wilkesiana tricolor, 20
Alteranthera amabilis, 21-22
Amaltas, 92
Amaranthus melancholicus, 92
Amaryllis, 53, 55
Ambroise verschaffelt, 21
Amiability, 51
Arundo donas, 107
Avoid the pink and magenta colours, 108

B

Balsams, 92
Beauty of Waltham, 68
Begin to move, 89
Beumontia grandiflora, 25
Bignonia vensuta, 93
Bignonias, 90
Blechnum, 40
Blechunum boreale, 41, 42
Boiling water, 99
Bombax malabaricum, 26, 92
Breathe freely, 35

C

Calamus roxburghii, 59
Carissa carandas, 51
Caryota urens, 59
Caudatum, 20
Centaurea cyanus, 34
Chandnee, 43
Chrysanthemum carinatum, 56
Chrysanthemums, 90, 102, 103
Consolation, 64
Cordillers of Spain, 46
Crystallize grasses, 99
Cystopteris, 40

D

Dodonea, 93

E

Eschscholtzia, 64
Eucharis lilies, 54

F

Fairest flowers of the season, 63
Fat, 60
Flat bonnet wire, 85
Flowers and gardens, 1-77
- acalyphas, 20
- achimens, 21
- *Alteranthera amabilis*, 21-22
- amaranthus, 22
- aristolochia, 23
- articles necessary for

garden use, 10
arundo donax, 23
– – versicolor, 23
asters, 22-23
balsams, 23
bamboos, 24
barry cornwall, 75
Bauhinia – Kuchnar, 25-26
Beumontia grandiflora, 25
Bombax malabaricum, 26
Bougainillea, 26
box (Sumatra box), 27
caladiums, 27-28
camphire (mehndee), 28-29
candy-tuft, 29-30
canes, 30-31
canna, 31
chrysanthemums, 31-33
conservatory, 12
coreopsis, 34
cornflowers, 34
crotons, 35
cyanotis, 35
Cyperus tenuifolius, 36
description of roses, 67
pink roses, 67
dodonea, 36
dorunta, 38
dracenas, 37-38
Edward's rose, 68
ferns, 38
flower-pots, 16-17
garden stands, 18-19
gardenia, 43
gardening book, 17-18
gardens on large scale, 5
gardens soils, 14-15
geraniums, 44
gilliflowers, 44
grass for lawn, 6-7, 44
Grevillea robusta, 45
gypsophila, 45
heliotrope, 46
hibiscus, 47
hollyhock, 47
Ipomea palmate, 49
ixora, 50
jasmine, 51
kuronda, 51
Legestroemia indica, 52
larkspur, 53
lawn, an absolute necessity, 2
lawn-mower, 7
laying our the ground, 2
lilies, 53
little talk about gardening, 1
mali, 5
many uses of Kerosine tins, 11-12
marguerite, 56
mehndee see camphire, 56
mignonetee, 56
mow, sweep, roll, water, 8
Nasturtium (tropaeolum), 57
oleanders, 58
oxalis, 58
palms, 59
pansies, 61
patunia, 61
pillar stands, 20
pinks, 63

pleasures of gardening, 1
plumbago, 64
poppies, 64
preparing ground for the lawn, 6
Quisqualis indica, 65
rosaries and rose-walks, 8
rose cuttings, 9
roses, 65
pink, 66
red, 66, 68
white, 66
yellow, 66
russellia, 71
saxifrage, 71
seed sowing, 15-16
selaginella, 72
shrubberies and side-walks, 3
snapdragon, 72
stone-roller, 7
suitable time of year, 3
sweet briar, 38
sweet-pea, 72
Tecoma grandiflora, 73
tecoma stands, 73
thunbergia, 73
tradecantiae discolour or bicolour, 74
trays, hanging baskets, 19
treatment of roses, 9
tropeolum see nasturtium, 74
verbenas, 74
Victor vardier, 68
violets, 75
wheat, 76
white roses, 69
work-yard enclosure, 3
yellow roses, 69

G

Garden soils, 15
Gardener's receipt book, 82
Gardeners, 81
Generous and devoted affection, 48
Geraniums, 90
Gilliflowers, 63
Goniopteris prolifera, 40
Gool Fanoos, 52
Grevillea robusta, 45, 85

H

Hedera helix, 49
Hedychium coronarium, 53, 54
Heliotropes, 90
Hints, 78-108
artificial coral, 82
baskets for plants and flowers, 79
bronze or colour grass, 83
caladiums, 101
canna, 102
caterpillars, 82
Christmas decorations, 100
chrysanthemums, 31-33, 90, 102
cold-weather flowers, 89
coleus, 101
colours for flower-stands, 86
celadon, 86
Etruscan pink, 86
coral varnish, 81
cut flowers fresh, 97
– sent as railway parcels, 98
delicate cuttings, 81

destroy maggots and worms, 83
dried ferns, 85
– grasses, 82
flower supports in vases, 80
– and foliage plants in the rains, 89
– for hospitals, 88
– fresh in the hot weather, 84-85
– in southern stations, 90
– in the hot weather, 89
frost foliage, 100
gardenia, 101
H. rose sinensis, 102
hibiscus, 101
honeysuckle, 102
Inga dulcis, 103
insects of plants, 81
– syringafolium, 103
labels, 84
marguerites, 103
minna lobata, 104
mirros, coloured glass, 104
moss baskets, 104
nasturtiums, 104
pack flowers for traveling, 98
pansies, 104
petunias, 105
phlox, 105
poppies, 105
pots for verandahs, 78
protection against frost, 79
– – vermin, 79
rid of insects, 81
roses, 89, 105
rustic supports, 80
scent sachets, 100
sorts of insect pests, 82
strains on flower vases, 96
Sumatra box, 27, 106
sweet-pea, 106
teak-tree blossoms, 106
tea-tables, 86
tradescantia, 107
varnish for rustic work, 80-81
verandah steps, 79
verbenas, 107
violets, 107
weeding cake decorations, 96
Yucca gloriosa, 107
zinnias, 108
Hirmajee, 17
Honeysuckle, 48

I

Indian garden, 62
Inga dulcis, 2, 48

J

Jaffery, 48
Jaman, 108
Jasmimum syringafolium, 103
Jasminum officinale, 103

K

Kar-khana, 4
Kentia Forsteriana, 59
Kerosine tins, 10
Kuchnar, 26
Kummul, 30
Kunkur, 13

L

Lagestroemia indica, 52
Language of flowers, 17
Lastrea, 40
Lathyrus odoratus, 72
Legestroemia indica, 52, 94
Livistona mauritiana, 59
Long journey, 98
Lord Morpeth, 51
Love at first sight, 34
Lunulatum, 20

M

Mehndee, 37, 65
Mina lobata, 57
Morning in winter, 60
Muses Elysium, 105

O

Oorchids, 94

P

Papaver alpinum, 45
Phlox drummonid, 62
Phoenix acaulis, 59
Pilea muscosa, 63
Pilea muscosa, 13
Polypodium, 40
Popular gardener, 81
Practical Gardening for Indian Amateurs, 17
Professor Howard, Entomologist, 82
Pure love, 63

R

Reseda odorate, 56
Rosary, 5
Rose cuttings, 89
Russelia juncea, 95

S

Sandwich Island creeper, 95
Schiller, 108
Shakespeare, 61
Short railway journey, 98, 99
Silk Oak, 45
Sloping bank, 76
Soorke, 2
Spluttered, 100
Stir up the surface of the soil, 9
Succession of sowings, 24
Sudden death, 42

T

Teberna Montana coronaria, 101
Tecoma stans, 108
Temple, Sir William, 1
Thing of beauty, 44
Thrinax argentea, 59
Time for gardening operations, 91
Tom Thumb, 57
Towards the light, 27
Transplanting ferns in the hot weather, 42
Treatment of roses, 89
Turkey red, 88

U

Umbrella fern, 36

V

Varnished side, 92
Virgil, 108